GW00502902

Qualifications and Credit Framework (QCF)
LEVEL 3 DIPLOMA IN ACCOUNTING

TEXT

Cash Management

2010 Edition

First edition July 2010

ISBN 9780 7517 8560 9

British Library Cataloguing-in-Publication Data
A catalogue record for this book is available from the British
Library

Published by

BPP Learning Media Ltd
BPP House
Aldine Place
London
W12 8AA

www.bpp.com/learningmedia

Printed in the United Kingdom

CONTENTS

INTRODUCTION

This is a time of great change for the AAT. From 1 July 2010 the AAT's assessments will fall within the **Qualifications and Credit Framework** and most papers will be assessed by way of an on demand **computer based assessment**. BPP Learning Media has reacted to this change by investing heavily to produce new ground breaking market leading resources. In particular, our **new suite of online resources** ensures that you are prepared for online testing by means of an online environment where tasks mimic the style of the AAT's assessment tasks.

The BPP Learning Media range of resources comprises:

- **Texts**, covering all the knowledge and understanding needed, with numerous illustrations of 'how it works', practical examples and tasks for you to use to consolidate your learning. The majority of tasks within the texts have been written in an interactive style that reflects the style of the online tasks the AAT will set. Texts are available in our traditional paper format and, in addition, as E-books which can be downloaded to your PC or laptop

- **Question Banks**, including additional learning questions plus the AAT's practice assessment and a number of other full practice assessments. Full answers to all questions and assessments, prepared by BPP Learning Media Ltd, are included. For the first time our question banks are available in an online environment which mimics the AAT's testing environment. This enables you to familiarise yourself with the environment in which you will be tested

- **Passcards,** which are handy pocket sized revision tools designed to fit in a handbag or briefcase to enable students to revise anywhere at anytime. All major points are covered in the passcards which have been designed to assist you in consolidating knowledge

- **Workbooks,** which have been designed to cover the units that are assessed by way of project/case study. The workbooks contain many practical tasks to assist in the learning process and also a sample assessment or project to work through

- **Lecturers' resources**, providing a further bank of tasks, answers and full practice assessments for classroom use, available separately only to lecturers whose colleges adopt BPP Learning Media material. The lecturers resources are available in both paper format and online in E-format

This Text for Cash Management has been written specifically to ensure comprehensive yet concise coverage of the AAT's new learning outcomes and assessment criteria. It is fully up to date as at June 2010 and reflects both the AAT's unit guide and the practice assessment provided by the AAT.

Each chapter contains:

- Clear, step by step explanation of the topic

- Logical progression and linking from one chapter to the next

- Numerous illustrations of 'how it works'

- Interactive tasks within the text of the chapter itself, with answers at the back of the book. In general, these tasks have been written in the interactive form that students will see in their real assessments

- Test your learning questions of varying complexity, again with answers supplied at the back of the book. In general these test questions have been written in the interactive form that students will see in their real assessments

The emphasis in all tasks and test questions is on the practical application of the skills acquired.

If you have any comments about this book, please e-mail suedexter@bpp.com or write to Sue Dexter, Publishing Director, BPP Learning Media Ltd, BPP House, Aldine Place, London W12 8AA.

Terminology

We refer to 'cash balance' in our examples of cash budgets. The assessor calls this 'bank balance'. The two terms mean the same thing in this text.

ASSESSMENT STRATEGY

The Principles of Cash Management and Cash Management units are combined for assessment purposes. **Students should attempt this paper after API/II as they will need knowledge of accruals/prepayments**.

The assessment is normally a two hour computer based assessment.

The assessment is divided into two sections, each consisting of six tasks, and will cover all of the learning outcomes and assessment criteria of the QCF Units Principles of Cash Management (knowledge) and Cash Management (skills).

Section 1 is concerned with the knowledge and techniques required for preparing cash budgets. This includes recognising the importance of cash and the relationship between cash and profit, forecasting income and expenditure using a variety of techniques and preparing a cash budget taking account of forecast information and expected timing patterns of cash flows.

Section 2 focuses on the skills needed for managing cash balances in accordance with organisational guidelines. This includes sensitivity analysis, cash flow monitoring, raising finance and investing surplus funds.

Students will normally be assessed by computer based assessment and will be required to demonstrate competence in both sections of the assessment.

Competency

Students will be required to demonstrate competence in both sections of the assessment. For the purpose of assessment the competency level for AAT assessment is set at 70 per cent. The level descriptor in the table below describes the ability and skills students at this level must successfully demonstrate to achieve competence.

QCF Level descriptor	Summary
	Achievement at level 3 reflects the ability to identify and use relevant understanding, methods and skills to complete tasks and address problems that, while well defined, have a measure of complexity. It includes taking responsibility for initiating and completing tasks and procedures as well as exercising autonomy and judgement within limited parameters. It also reflects awareness of different perspectives or approaches within an area of study or work.

Knowledge and understanding

- Use factual, procedural and theoretical understanding to complete tasks and address problems that, while well defined, may be complex and non-routine

- Interpret and evaluate relevant information and ideas

- Be aware of the nature of the area of study or work

- Have awareness of different perspectives or approaches within the area of study or work

Application and action

- Address problems that, while well defined, may be complex and non–routine

- Identify, select and use appropriate skills, methods and procedures

- Use appropriate investigation to inform actions

- Review how effective methods and actions have been

Autonomy and accountability

- Take responsibility for initiating and completing tasks and procedures, including, where relevant, responsibility for supervising or guiding others

- Exercise autonomy and judgement within limited parameters

AAT UNIT GUIDE

Cash Management

Introduction

The Principles of Cash Management and Cash Management units are combined for assessment purposes. The purpose of this document is to describe what is assessable for each of these criteria.

Please read this document in conjunction with the standards for all relevant units.

The purpose of the unit

Organisations that fail to manage their liquid resources appropriately expose themselves to a higher risk of failure than organisations that effectively manage their cash. This Unit is designed to equip accounting technicians not only with an understanding of the theoretical principles of good cash management but also with the practical skills to undertake the preparation of cash budgets using a range of financial information, to select appropriate methods of financing cash shortfalls and to recommend suitable investment for surplus funds.

Terminology

Students should be familiar with interchangeable terminology including IAS and UK GAAP.

Learning objectives

In the Principles of Cash Management (Knowledge) unit learners develop an understanding of the principles of managing cash balances and deficits within an organisation. Learners will understand and be able to advise on options available for both raising finance and investing surplus cash. Any advice offered should not be detrimental to the cash flow of normal business activities and should minimise risk to the organisation.

In the Cash Management (Skills) unit learners develop the skills necessary for managing cash balances to ensure the ongoing liquidity of an organisation. Learners will demonstrate these skills through the forecasting of income and expenditure and the preparation of cash budgets that enable informed decision-making regarding both the borrowing and investing of surplus funds.

Learning outcomes

There are two QCF units involved. Each is divided into component learning outcomes, which in turn comprise a number of assessment criteria.

Learning outcome	Assessment criteria	Covered in chapter
Understand how the external environment impacts on how an organisation manages cash assets	Explain how recording and accounting practices may vary in different parts of the organisation	**1, 6**
	Take accounts of trends in the economic and financial environment in managing cash balances	
	Identify statutory and other regulations relating to the management of cash balances in different types of organisations	
	Explain how government monetary policies affect an organisation's treasury function	
Be able to make informed decisions regarding the management of cash balances within an organisation	Identify the characteristics of the main types of cash receipts and payments of regular revenue receipts, capital receipts, exceptional receipts and payments and drawings	**2, 6**
	Identify statutory and other regulations relating to the management of cash balances in different types of organisations	
	Explain how an organisation can raise finance from a bank through overdrafts and loans, and the basic terms and conditions associated with each of these types of financing	
	Describe how an organisation's principles of cash management will be determined by their specific financial regulations, guidelines and security procedures	

Understand a range of accounting and other business techniques used to improve the efficiency of cash management	Identify the principles of liquidity management	**1, 2, 4**
	Describe the relationship between cash flow accounting and accounting for income and expenditure	
	Explain techniques that can be used for estimating future trends including moving averages and allowances for inflation	
Prepare forecasts of income and expenditure for a given accounting period	Explain the effects of lagged receipts and payments on an organisation's cash management	**3, 4, 5**
	Determine the likely pattern of cash flows over the accounting period and anticipate any exceptional receipts and payments	
	Explain techniques that can be used for estimating future trends including moving averages and allowances for inflation	
	Ensure that forecasts of future cash payments and receipts agree with known income and expenditure trends	
	Identify the component parts of cash budgets and how these are presented to aid decision making	
	Prepare cash budgets and clearly indicate net requirements	
Use forecasts to monitor the cash flow within the organisation	Monitor cash receipts and payments against budgeted cash flow	**8**
	Identify significant deviations from cash budget and take corrective action within organisational policies	

Use cash balances effectively	Explain how an organisation can raise finance from a bank through overdrafts and loans, and the basic terms and conditions associated with each of these types of financing	**6, 7**
	Manage cash, overdrafts and loans in order to maintain an adequate level of liquidity in line with forecasts	
	Anticipate cash requirements and arrange overdrafts and loan facilities on the most favourable terms available	
	Explain different types of investment, the risks and terms and conditions associated with them including certificates of deposit, government securities, local authority short loans and shares	
	Identify ways to manage risk and exposure when investing, to minimise potential losses to the organisation	
	Observe the organisation's financial regulations and security procedures	
	Invest surplus funds according to organisational policy and within defined authorisation limits	**6, 7**

Delivery guidance: Cash management

This section provides detailed delivery guidance covering assessable topics and the depth and breadth to which these topics should be taught and learnt.

The term cash in this Unit is used to include bank accounts as well as coins and notes and cash payments include cheque payments, BACS, direct debits and standing orders.

The effective management of cash is not something that can be undertaken in isolation or without an awareness of the general financial environment in which organisations operate. Therefore it is important that learners have a basic awareness of how the banking sector is structured, the relationship between different financial institutions and understand that legal relationships exist between lenders and borrowers. Learners should also be introduced to the sort of financial terminology which they could encounter in the workplace such as fixed and floating charges, brokers, money markets. Though these areas are not specifically assessable they are essential background knowledge.

Assessment tasks may use some technical financial terminology however learners will only be expected to display knowledge or understanding of terms that are specifically noted in the delivery guidance and standards as assessable. The use of other terms will simply be to add reality to a task and the ability to undertake the task in a competent manner will not depend upon any detailed knowledge of such terminology.

Assessment tasks may relate to a range of different organisations including sole traders, partnerships and limited companies. Learners will not be expected to have any prior knowledge of the structure or accounting regulations of these organisations as they will simply be used as a background setting to enable assessment. Receipts and payments that might be organisation specific, for example, corporation tax, could be used in tasks but learners will simply be required to treat these cash flows in accordance with the instructions in the assessment data.

Liquidity (LO3)

Assessment criteria:

3.4K   Identify the principles of liquidity management

Adequate liquidity is often a key factor in contributing to the success or failure of trading organisations. Learners need to understand that cash is part of the working capital of the business and that the time taken to convert inventory, receivables and payables into cash affects the liquidity position of the organisation. Liquidity management involves monitoring cash flows through the working capital cycle, understanding that different types of cash flows have different timing patterns, using cash budgets to forecast and monitor the organisation's liquidity position, arranging finance to cover expected cash shortfalls and investing cash surpluses to achieve maximum returns. A key principle of liquidity management is being able to recognise the indicators of possible future liquidity problems which include overtrading and overcapitalisation.

Through practical tasks, learners should be able to demonstrate they understand:

- The meaning of liquidity and be able to identify different forms of liquid assets.

- How the circulation of working capital is demonstrated by the cash cycle.

- Why liquidity/cash is important to a business both for daily operations and for its ability to meet future financial obligations.

- The key principles of liquidity management.

- The nature of, the dangers associated with and the indicator signs of overtrading and overcapitalisation.

The relationship between cash flow accounting and accounting for income and expenditure (LO3)

Assessment criteria:

3.3K   Describe the relationship between cash flow accounting and accounting for income and expenditure

Although this Unit is primarily concerned with cash flows for an organisation learners need to understand how cash flow accounting relates to accounting (financial) statements which are prepared to show the income and expenditure (profitability) of an organisation. Financial statements are prepared using accounting adjustments such as accruals, prepayments and depreciation and therefore do not show the cash position of an organisation. Information required for the preparation of a cash budget comes from a variety of sources which may include an Income Statement (Profit and Loss Account). Knowledge of how figures from financial accounting statements can be adjusted to reverse the effect of accounting adjustments and thereby find the cash transactions to be included in a cash budget is essential.

Cash flow statements prepared under FRS 1 are not assessable in this Unit.

Through practical tasks, learners should be able to demonstrate they understand:

- The difference between cash flow accounting and accounting for income and expenditure and the importance of distinguishing cash from profit.

- How the value of cash transactions can be calculated by adjusting figures in the Income Statement to reverse the effect of accounting adjustments such as accruals, prepayments and depreciation.

Cash receipts, cash payments and the likely pattern of cash flows (LO 1, 2, 3, 4)

Assessment criteria:

1.2K   *Explain how recording and accounting practices may vary in different parts of the organisation*

2.1K   *Identify the characteristics of the main types of cash receipts and payments of regular revenue receipts, capital receipts, exceptional receipts and payments and drawings*

3.2K   *Explain the effects of lagged receipts and payments upon an organisation's cash management*

1.1S   *Determine the likely pattern of cash flows over the accounting period and anticipate any exceptional receipts and payments*

Effective liquidity management depends upon understanding that cash receipts and payments can be categorised in a number of ways according to their main characteristics and their differing patterns of cash flow. A cash budget needs to recognise different types of receipts and payments and incorporate a variety of payment patterns that arise both from the nature of the receipt or payment and from the effects of lagging.

In order to be able to determine the likely pattern of cash flows over a period it is necessary to understand the possible sources of information within an organisation and to recognise that transactions may be recorded in different ways in different parts of the organisation.

Through practical tasks, learners should be able to demonstrate they understand:

- The characteristics of regular, capital and exceptional cash receipts and give examples for each type of cash flow. Regular (operational) receipts are those that are expected to occur frequently and arise from the operating activities of the organisation. Capital receipts are those relating to proceeds from the disposal of non-current assets (fixed assets). Exceptional receipts are those that are not expected to reoccur on a regular basis and do not arise from the operating activities of the organisation however they could be large and thus materially impact the cash position of an organisation.

- The characteristics of regular, capital and exceptional cash payments as well as drawings and give examples for each type of cash flow. Regular (operational) cash payments are those that are expected to occur frequently and arise from the operating activities of the organisation. Capital payments relate to the acquisition of non-current assets. Exceptional payments are those that are not expected to recur on a regular basis and drawings are amounts withdrawn from the organisation by its owners and could be either regular or irregular in nature. Exceptional items and irregular drawings could materially impact the cash position of the organisation.

- How recording and accounting practices may vary in different parts of the organisation resulting in a variety of sources of information being available for determining likely patterns of cash flow.

- The effect of lagged receipts and payments on an organisation's cash flow and cash management.

- How to use information obtained from a range of sources within an organisation to determine the likely pattern of different types of cash receipts and cash payments for inclusion in a cash budget. Given the potential impact of exceptional receipts and payments on the cash position of an organisation these types of cash flows should be anticipated to ensure that they are included in the cash budget in the correct period so that their likely effect can be assessed.

- How to determine the likely pattern of cash receipts and payments incorporating the effects of lagging.

Forecasting future cash receipts and payments (LO 3, 4)

Assessment criteria:

3.5K   *Explain techniques that can be used for estimating future trends including moving averages and allowance for inflation*

1.2S   *Ensure forecasts of future cash payments and receipts agree with known income and expenditure trends*

3.2S   *Take account of trends in the economic and financial environment in managing cash balances*

Known income and expenditure trends must be considered and incorporated into estimates of future cash receipts and payments that are to be included in a cash budget. There are a variety of statistical techniques that could be used to forecast future cash receipts and payments but this Unit focuses on moving averages and allowance for inflation. Previous income and expenditure trends could also be derived from graphical information or a review of historical results where this indicates simple, regular increases or decreases. Learners must be able to use these techniques to forecast future cash receipts and payments.

Through practical tasks, learners should be able to demonstrate they understand:

- How moving averages (time series analysis) can be used to identify past trends in volume or value which can then be used to estimate future trends.

- How to use moving averages to identify the basic trend of income or expenditure and use this trend to forecast future cash receipts and payments. Calculations will be based on odd-points (i.e. 3-point, 5-point etc) only and therefore calculations including centred averages will not be required. Learners should be able to calculate period variations (seasonal variations) by finding the difference between the trend and the actual figure and use this to forecast income or expenditure. Any variations will be cyclical.

- How to forecast future cash receipts and payments based on known trends by calculating and using an average monthly change.

- A trend from graphical information and use the trend to forecast future cash receipts and payments.

- The need to make allowances for inflation and describe the techniques that could be applied when estimating future trends of income and expenditure, for example the application of percentage increases and the use of index numbers.

- How to forecast future cash receipts and payments making allowances for known trends in inflation.

- The inherent problems of forecasting figures and how these can impact on the usefulness of a cash budget.

Prepare cash budgets and indicate the net cash position (LO 3, 4)

Assessment criteria:

3.1K   *Identify the component parts of cash budgets and how these are presented to aid decision making*

1.3S   *Prepare cash budgets and clearly indicate net cash requirements*

Cash budgets provide decision makers with an effective tool for cash management therefore learners who are able to accurately prepare a cash budget from a variety of information will be equipped with a valuable practical skill.

The preparation of a cash budget will necessarily require learners to use a range of information presented in a variety of ways depending upon the nature of the organisation and its activities. At this level learners will be expected to be able to extract information from data that is presented in different ways. However, clear instructions will be provided in assessment tasks so that a detailed knowledge of the preparation of budgets (other than cash), the composition of financial statements or the specific structure of an organisation will not be required.

Cash budgets are prepared using assumptions about the nature of cash flows. It is important to understand that net cash requirements will be affected by changes in those assumptions and that revised cash budgets will need to be prepared.

Through practical tasks, learners should be able to demonstrate they understand:

- The component parts of cash budgets. Cash budgets do not have a statutory format and organisations may chose to present information in different ways but for a cash budget to be useful it should incorporate the following:
  - Analysis of sources of receipts leading to total receipts for the period
  - Analysis of the sources of payments leading to total payments for the period
  - Net cash flow for the period
  - Bank balance bought forward
  - Bank balance carried forward

- The uses of a cash budget and explain how the format of a cash budget can aid decision making by showing the composition and timing of receipts and payments and changes in the net cash position.

- How to calculate sales receipts for inclusion in a cash budget after accounting for early settlement discounts, sales price fluctuations, bad debts and the effect of lagging.

- How to calculate purchase payments for inclusion in a cash budget after accounting for early settlement discounts, purchase price fluctuations and the effect of lagging.

- How to calculate non-sales receipts and non-purchase payments for inclusion in the cash budget from a variety of information incorporating different payment patterns. Clear instructions will be given in the assessment data regarding the payment pattern of these types of cash flows.

- How to prepare a cash budget for a number of periods for a new or an existing organisation, clearly indicating the net cash position at the end of each period. Cash budget figures should be rounded to whole £'s following normal rounding conventions.

- How to calculate and incorporate bank interest received and bank interest paid into a cash budget.

- How to prepare revised cash budgets to quantify changes in the net cash requirements that result when original assumptions regarding volumes, values and payment patterns change.

Anticipate and manage cash shortages by raising suitable finance (LO 1, 2, 6)

Assessment criteria:

1.4K   Identify statutory and other regulations relating to the management of cash balances in different types of organisations

2.2K   Explain how an organisation can raise finance from a bank through overdrafts and loans, and the basic terms and conditions associated with each of these types of financing

3.3S   Manage cash, overdrafts and loans in order to maintain an adequate level of liquidity in line with cash forecasts

3.4S   Anticipate cash requirements and arrange overdraft and loan facilities on the most favourable terms available

A cash budget is one method that an organisation can use to anticipate future cash shortages based on their forecast activities. A cash budget provides a periodic forecast of net cash positions that will enable management to select and arrange suitable financing options to cover any cash shortages.

Organisations can raise finance from a range of sources but this Unit only requires knowledge of finance raised from banks in the form of overdrafts and loans. Learners need to understand that all financing options have differing terms and conditions attached to them and that there are a number of factors that need to be considered before recommending a suitable form of finance. Different organisations may have established regulations, policies and guidelines governing the sources of, and terms under which, finance can be raised. An important point to recognise is that those charged with liquidity management owe a fiduciary duty of care to the owners of the organisation.

Through practical tasks, learners should be able to demonstrate they understand:

- Statutory and other organisational regulations and guidelines that relate to the management of cash balances. Learners will not be expected to identify specific statutory regulations but must be aware that some organisations are governed by mandatory regulations that need to be adhered to e.g. limited companies through the Companies Act, and public sector organisations.

- Financing can be obtained from banks in the form of loans and overdrafts.

- The main features of overdrafts and loans available from a bank, including interest rates (fixed, variable and capped), fees, time period, repayment structure, security (personal guarantee, fixed and floating charges), advantages and disadvantages. Explain the nature, purpose and content of facility letters.

- How to use a cash budget to anticipate financing requirements and arrange overdraft and loan facilities on the most favourable terms available.

- What is required in order to make recommendations for financing cash shortfalls identified by a cash budget, selecting the most appropriate form of financing for a particular project considering the time period, purpose and amount of finance needed. Recommendations should consider the possibility of combining different types of financing options to maintain an adequate level of liquidity at the lowest possible cost and to meet the organisation's own guidelines and regulations.

Use forecasts to monitor cash flow within an organisation, identify significant variations and take corrective action (LO 5)

Assessment criteria:

2.1S   Monitor cash receipts and payments against budgeted cash flow

2.2S   Identify significant deviations from cash budget and take corrective action within organisational policies

In addition to being a tool for predicting cash shortfalls and cash surpluses, a cash budget can be used to monitor and control cash inflows and outflows. Cash management is not simply about being able to prepare a cash budget it also involves being able to quantify deviations from budget and to identify possible reasons for those deviations so that appropriate courses of action can be taken.

Through practical tasks, learners should be able to demonstrate they understand:

- Compare actual cash flows with forecast cash flows to calculate deviations (variances). Standard costing variance analysis is not assessable at this level.

- Summarise deviations from cash budget by reconciling budgeted cash flow with actual cash flow.

- Identify possible reasons for differences between budgeted cash flows and actual cash flows (both adverse and favourable) so that corrective action can be suggested. Recommended action must have regard to the impact of such actions on the cash position of the organisation and on organisational policies. Ensure that possible courses of action are matched with the nature and cause of cash variances.

Managing surplus funds (LO 1, 2, 3, 6)

Assessment criteria:

1.1K   Explain how government monetary policies affect an organisation's treasury function

1.3K   Describe how an organisation's principles of cash management will be determined by their specific financial regulations, guidelines and security procedures

1.4K   *Identify statutory and other regulations relating to the management of cash balances in different types of organisations*

2.3K   *Explain different types of investment, the risks and terms and conditions associated with them, including certificates of deposit, government securities, local authority short loans and shares*

3.6K   *Identify the ways to manage risk and exposure when investing, to minimise potential losses to the organisation*

3.1S   *Observe the organisation's financial regulations and security procedures*

3.5S   *Invest surplus funds according to organisational policy and within defined authorisation limits*

As well as being able to select suitable finance for dealing with cash shortages organisations need to utilise cash surpluses in the most appropriate manner to ensure that they receive maximum return for minimum risk. Different organisations have different regulations and guidelines governing investment and learners must take these into account when making recommendations.

Through practical tasks, learners should be able to demonstrate they understand:

- What is meant by the term 'treasury function'.

- Explain how the government's monetary policy in controlling the supply of money in the economy, and the effect of this on the rate of inflation and interest rates, impacts an organisation's treasury function.

- That different organisations will have their own financial regulations, guidelines and security procedures (including physical security) that must be observed when considering possible courses of action and making recommendations. Describe how these regulations, guidelines and procedures affect the organisation's principles of cash management.

- Different types of investments and the nature, risks, cost, terms and conditions associated with them including certificates of deposit, government securities, local authority short term loans and shares.

- Ways that an organisation could manage risk and exposure when investing surplus funds to try to ensure that potential losses are minimised.

What is required in order to make recommendations for investing surplus funds having regard to the organisation's policies and procedures, internal regulations, attitude towards risk, return, termination costs, realisation and authorisation limits.

chapter 1:
LIQUIDITY

chapter coverage 📖

In this opening chapter of the Text for Level 3 Cash Management we consider the importance of liquidity to a business and how the working capital cycle plays a part in the liquidity of the business. The topics that are covered are:

✍   What is meant by liquidity

✍   Working capital and the cash cycle

✍   Principles of liquidity management

✍   Over-trading and over-capitalisation

LIQUIDITY

LIQUIDITY is the ability of a company to pay its suppliers on time, meet its operational costs such as wages and salaries and to pay any longer-term outstanding amounts such as loan repayments. Adequate liquidity is often a key factor in contributing to the success or failure of a business. The liquidity of a business is the availability of cash or assets which can easily be converted into cash therefore liquidity is not just about holding cash in hand or in a bank current account as there are also other liquid assets. These include:

- Deposit account balances

- Short-term investments which can easily be sold and converted into cash

- Trade receivables (debtors) – although it may be some time before the monies are received

- Inventories (stocks) – although these of course must be manufactured/sold before they can be converted into cash

Liquidity is a measure of how safe the business is in terms of its cash availability. Even if a business is profitable it must also have enough cash to pay amounts due when they become payable.

Cash is the most liquid of assets and is part of the working capital of the business. It is also important to realise that the time taken to convert inventory (stocks) and trade receivables (debtors) into cash and the time taken to pay trade payables (creditors) affects the liquidity position of the business.

Working capital

We will now consider the WORKING CAPITAL of the business in more detail.

Working capital is the total of the current assets of the business less the current liabilities. It is the amount of money invested in inventories (stocks) and trade receivables (debtors) less the credit allowed from trade payables (creditors) and it is a necessary part of most business's investment.

The component elements of working capital are constantly changing as the diagram below illustrates:

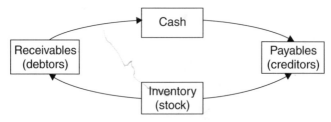

- Inventory (stock) is turned into trade receivables (debtors) when it is sold

- Inventory (stock) is purchased on credit which means we have trade payables (creditors)

- Trade receivables (debtors) will eventually be turned into cash

- Cash will be used to pay trade payables (creditors)

The working capital cycle can be determined by looking at each of the individual components of working capital – inventory (stock), receivables (debtors) and payables (creditors).

Inventory (stock) turnover

We will start with inventory (stock). It is useful for management to have an indication of how long inventories (stocks) are being held. In some businesses inventory (stock) must be sold, or turned over, quickly, for example if the inventory (stock) is made up of perishable foods. However, in other businesses inventory (stock) may be held for some considerable time before it is sold (eg in the construction industry).

A business needs to control how long inventory (stock) is being held as capital is tied up in the inventory (stock) while it is waiting to be sold. Therefore an INVENTORY (STOCK) TURNOVER ratio can be calculated to show the length of time that inventory (stock) is held in the business.

$$\text{Inventory (stock) turnover} = \frac{\text{Average inventory (stock)}}{\text{Cost of sales}} \times 365$$

This will indicate the number of days on average that the inventory (stock) is being held before sale. You will note that 'average inventory (stock)' has been used here. This is calculated as:

$$\text{Average inventory (stock)} = \frac{\text{Opening inventory (stock)} + \text{Closing inventory (stock)}}{2}$$

In some computer based tests you may not have information about the opening inventory (stock) and therefore the closing inventory (stock) figure can be used in the inventory (stock) turnover calculation rather than average inventory (stock). However, if the opening inventory (stock) figure is available then use average inventory (stock) in your calculation.

Receivables' (Debtors') collection period

The RECEIVABLES' (DEBTORS') COLLECTION PERIOD ratio, also known as receivables' (debtors') days, is a measure that shows how long it is taking for the receivables (debtors) of the business to pay.

$$\text{Receivables' (debtors') collection period} = \frac{\text{Trade receivables (debtors)}}{\text{Credit sales}} \times 365 \text{ days}$$

One problem may be with the use of year-end receivables (debtors) as these may not be representative of the average receivables (debtors) throughout the year. Therefore - if possible - use the average of opening and closing receivables (debtors) but in computer based tests it is rare for this information to be available.

Payables' (Creditors') payment period

The PAYABLES' (CREDITORS') PAYMENT PERIOD ratio, or payables' (creditors') days indicates how long a business takes to pay its trade payables (creditors).

$$\text{Payables' (creditors') payment period} = \frac{\text{Trade payables (creditors)}}{\text{Credit purchases}} \times 365 \text{ days}$$

In some cases there will not be a separate figure for purchases, in which case cost of sales must be used even though this is not as appropriate. In many computer based tests only cost of sales information will be available. If the average of opening and closing payables (creditors) is accessible this is better than just the closing figure but normally only the closing figure will be given.

HOW IT WORKS

Set out below are the Income Statement (profit and loss account) and Statement of Financial Position (balance sheet) for Hampton Manufacturing:

Hampton Manufacturing

Income Statement for the year ended

30 September 20X8

	£
Turnover	1,350,400
Cost of sales	837,200
Gross profit	513,200
Less: expenses	274,000
Operating profit	239,200

Hampton Manufacturing

Statement of Financial Position as at 30 September 20X8

	£	£
Non-current assets (Fixed assets)		2,428,300
Current assets:		
Inventory (Stock)	156,300	
Receivables (Debtors)	225,000	
Bank	10,200	
	391,500	
Payables (Creditors)	(169,800)	
Net current assets		221,700
		2,650,000
Capital		2,000,000
Retained earnings		650,000
		2,650,000

We will now calculate the individual working capital ratios.

Inventory (stock) turnover $\quad=\quad \dfrac{\text{Inventory (stock)}}{\text{Cost of sales}} \times 365$

$$= \frac{£156,300}{£837,200} \times 365$$

$$= 68 \text{ days}$$

Receivables' (debtors') collection period $\quad=\quad \dfrac{\text{Trade receivables (debtors)}}{\text{Credit sales}} \times 365$

$$= \frac{£225,000}{£1,350,400} \times 365$$

$$= 61 \text{ days}$$

Payables' (creditors') payment period $\quad=\quad \dfrac{\text{Trade payables (creditors)}}{\text{Cost of sales}} \times 365$

$$= \frac{£169,800}{£837,200} \times 365$$

$$= 74 \text{ days}$$

Task 1

A business has opening inventory (stock) of £13,500 and closing inventory (stock) of £17,000. Purchases during the year were £99,000.

What is the inventory (stock) turnover period in days?

A   50 days

B   56 days

C   63 days

D   112 days

$$\frac{13,500 + 17,000}{2} = \frac{15,250}{99,000} \times 365$$

$$= 56 \text{ DAYS}$$

Working capital cycle

The WORKING CAPITAL CYCLE or CASH CYCLE measures the period of time between the time cash is paid out for raw materials and the time cash is received in from customers for goods sold.

(a)   A firm buys raw materials, probably on credit.

(b)   It holds the raw materials for some time in stores before being issued to the production department and turned into an item of finished goods.

(c)   The finished goods might be kept in a warehouse for some time before they are eventually sold to customers.

(d)   By this time, the firm will probably have paid for the raw materials purchased.

(e)   If customers buy the goods on credit, it will be some time before the cash from the sales is eventually received.

The working capital cycle or cash cycle of a business in days is calculated as follows:

	Days
Inventory (stock) turnover period	X
Receivables' (debtors') collection period	X
	X
Less: payables' (creditors') payment period	(X)
Working capital cycle	X

For Hampton the working capital cycle is as follows:

	Days
Inventory (stock) turnover period	68
Receivables' (debtors') collection period	61
	129
Less: payables' (creditors') payment period	(74)
Working capital cycle	55

Task 2

A business has inventory (stock) turnover of 84 days, a receivables' (debtors') collection period of 51 days and a payables' (creditors') payment period of 43 days.

The working capital cycle in days is:

A   10 days

B   76 days

C   92 days

D   178 days

84 + 51 − 43

PRINCIPLES OF LIQUIDITY MANAGEMENT

Liquidity management is more than simply cash management. It is about control of not just cash but also inventory (stock), receivables (debtors) and payables (creditors). The shorter the working capital cycle the sooner cash is received and can be used elsewhere in the business. For this syllabus we are concerned principally with cash management. The three main principles to be considered are profitability, liquidity and security.

In the context of cash management; **profitability** relates specifically to how the firm manages its cash in order to minimise costs and maintain a return.

Liquidity can refer to the ease with which something can be converted into cash for use. Cash is the most 'liquid' asset of all. A short-term investment can be sold. Some accounts require notice. Buildings and property might be very illiquid, in that they are difficult to sell and convert into cash.

Security is the principle that cash and credit transactions should not involve the company in any undue risk.

(a)   Notes and coins should be secure from theft.

(b)   Cheques and electronic systems should be secure from fraud.

(c)   Short-term investments should be such that the firm does not stand to risk heavy losses through falls in value. Shares can fall in price.

There is a relationship between risk and return. Generally speaking safer investments offer lower returns. (This is considered in more detail in Chapter 7 of this Text.)

HOW IT WORKS

At the end of month 1, Bloggs Co finds it has cash balances surplus to requirements of £1,000, for which it has no conceivable use at the moment.

(a)   It can leave it in the bank current account, where it will earn no interest.

(b)   It can invest it in a deposit account where it will earn interest of £20 in month 2, provided the bank is given a *week's* notice should Bloggs require the money.

(c)   It can buy shares in Gamma Co. At the beginning of the month the shares in Gamma Co were worth £1,000 and at the end of the month, they were worth £1,040. It costs £10 to buy and sell the shares.

(d)   It can go to the stock market and buy some shares in Delta Co for a month. The value of a share can go down as well as up. It costs £10 in total to buy and sell the shares. At the beginning of the month the shares were worth £1,000 and at the end of the month they were worth £995.

Determine the best use of funds.

	Current Account (a)	Deposit account (b)	Gamma (c)	Delta (d)
Cash invested	(1,000)	(1,000)	(1,000)	(1,000)
Interest	–	20	–	–
Principal/sale proceeds	1,000	1,000	1,040	995
Transaction costs	–	–	(10)	(10)
Profit/(loss)	–	20	30	(15)

Gamma is the most profitable, but shares are more risky than the current or deposit accounts, as the example of Delta demonstrates.

Bloggs would be foolish simply to let the cash pile up and earn no money, even if investing is not the company's main business. At the same time, it must be careful to balance the risk of a course of action, such as investing in shares, with the profit. Although (a) earns nothing, the cash will be on hand **immediately** if needed.

We will look at these principles in more detail later in this Text.

OVER-TRADING AND OVER-CAPITALISATION

If sales turnover increases then this will often require increases in both inventories (stock) and trade receivables (debtors). The business may be able to gain additional credit from its trade payables (creditors) but in the absence of that, it may have to raise funds to finance this expansion.

Care should be taken by any expanding business to ensure that it does not get into an OVER-TRADING position. Over-trading is where a business expands more quickly than its funds will allow. The eventual result of over-trading is that the business does not have enough underlying funds to pay all of the business debts as they fall due and it may well end up as a bankrupt business.

Symptoms of over-trading

Revenue

Current/non-current (fixed) assets

Inventory (stock)
Receivables (debtors)
> Sales

SYMPTOMS OF OVER-TRADING

Current and quick ratios

Current liabilities
> Current assets

Assets financed by credit and not proprietors' capital

Over-capitalisation and working capital

OVER-CAPITALISATION is where there are excessive inventories (stock), receivables (debtors) and cash and very few payables (creditors). There is an over-investment by the business in current assets and working capital is excessive.

CHAPTER OVERVIEW

- Liquidity is the ability of a business to meet its payments as and when they are due.

- The most liquid asset of all is cash but other major assets may be bank deposits, investments, inventory (stock) and receivables (debtors).

- Working capital is made up of inventory (stock), receivables (debtors) and payables (creditors) and the working capital or cash cycle is an important indicator of the liquidity of a business.

- Liquidity management or cash management is concerned with profitability, liquidity and security.

- Over-trading and over-capitalisation can both be detected by considering the working capital ratios and the working capital cycle.

Keywords

Liquidity – the ability of a business to pay the amounts it owes as and when they fall due

Working capital – the total of the current assets of a business less its current liabilities

Inventory (stock) turnover period – the amount of time that inventory (stock) is being held by a business

Receivables' (debtors') collection period – the amount of time that it takes for trade receivables (debtors) to pay the amounts that they owe

Payables' (creditors') payment period – the amount of time it takes for a business to pay its trade payables (creditors)

The working capital cycle or **cash cycle** – the period of time between cash being paid for raw materials and cash being received from customers for goods sold

Over-trading – where a business expands more quickly than its funds allow

Over-capitalisation – where there is over-investment in working capital by a business

TEST YOUR LEARNING

Test 1

A business had sales of £790,000 during the year and cost of sales of £593,000. Inventory (stock) at the year end was valued at £68,000, receivables (debtors) were £102,000 and trade payables (creditors) were £57,000.

What is the working capital/cash cycle of the business?

A   30 days
B   40 days
C   54 days
D   124 days

Handwritten working:
$$\frac{68,000}{593,000} \times 365 = 42$$
$$+$$
$$\frac{102,000}{790000} \times 365 = 47$$
$$\frac{57,000}{593,000} \times 365 = 35$$

Test 2

Select the three most liquid assets that most businesses are likely to have from the list below.

■

■

■

Inventory (stock) of raw materials
Receivables (debtors)
Fleet of cars used in the business
Cash in hand
Business computers
Bank deposit account
Business head office
Investment in shares
Bank current account
Inventory (stock) of finished goods

Test 3

Selecting from the picklist, complete the following sentence.

The **three** main principles of the management of liquidity are [security/ethics/type of business invested in/liquidity/management preferences/profitability]

Test 4

A business has high levels of current assets but only small amounts of trade payables (creditors). What is this an example of? (Tick the appropriate answer)

Over-trading   ☐

Over-capitalisation   ☑

chapter 2:
CASH FLOW AND PROFIT

chapter coverage 📖

Although this Unit is primarily concerned with cash flows for an organisation, it is important to understand how cash flow accounting and the actual financial statements (Income Statement (profit and loss account) and Statement of Financial Position (balance sheet)) of a business are related. The topics that are covered are:

🖎 The difference between cash flow accounting and the accounting for income and expenditure

🖎 Cash and credit transactions

🖎 Calculating cash flows from financial statement information

CASH AND THE BUSINESS

When you think about a business the first question that you might reasonably ask about that business is 'Is it profitable?'. The aim of most businesses is, of course, to make a profit for its owners whether the business is that of a sole trader, a partnership or a company making profits for its shareholders.

If a business is profitable this means that it is making more by selling its goods or services than it is expending on the purchase of goods and the payment of expenses. However, profit is not always enough! In order for a business to succeed it must have cash in its bank account (or an agreed overdraft with its bank) in order to pay all of its costs and expenses as they fall due. If not the business could be in trouble and might eventually flounder. This is the liquidity position which we considered in Chapter 1.

HOW IT WORKS

Jo Kennedy has just set up a jewellery, gifts and cards business. She buys in materials, makes the jewellery, gifts and cards and then sells them to a few private customers but largely to a small number of retail outlets. She started the business on 1 March with £1,000 in her business bank account and during that month wrote cheques for materials for £800.

Jo felt that she had a good month in March as she made sales to private customers totalling £300 and further sales of £900 to various retail outlets. The private customers paid either by cash or cheque and Jo paid these into the business bank account immediately. However, the retail customers were not prepared to pay the amount they owed until May.

In April Jo needs to replenish her inventory (stock) of materials at a cost of £800 and to pay for two months rent on her studio totalling £350. How will she be able to do this?

	March £	April £	May £
Opening balance	1,000	500	(650)
Payments	(800)	(1,150)	
Receipts from private trade	300		
Receipts from retailers			900
Closing balance	500	(650)	250

By the end of March Jo still has £500 in the business bank account but her payments due in April are £1,150. Although there is £900 receivable in May from her March retail sales, without substantial cash receipts from private sales in April Jo will either not have enough money to continue in business or must approach her bank for a substantial overdraft.

This illustrates that in order to carry on in business it is important not only to be profitable but also to have the cash available to meet the business payments when they fall due.

Cash and profit

The previous simple example shows that there is a distinct difference between making a profit and having available cash. So now we will consider the reasons for the difference between profit and cash.

The accruals concept

The profit for a period is calculated using the accruals concept. Under the ACCRUALS CONCEPT revenue from sales and the cost of goods and expenses are accounted for in the period in which they are earned or incurred rather than in the period in which the cash is received or paid. Therefore, even though a business may appear to have made a profit in a period it may not yet have the cash to show for it.

Non-cash expenses

Generally expenses of a business will reduce the amount of cash that the business has as these expenses will have to be paid for. However there are some expenses which have no affect on cash at all, NON-CASH EXPENSES. The most obvious of these is the annual depreciation charge on non-current (fixed) assets. Although this is an expense of the business it is not an amount of cash leaving the business.

Receipts/payments not affecting profit

Many businesses will find that on occasions they have receipts of cash into the business which do not affect profit. For example, if a sole trader pays more capital into the business or a company issues additional shares for cash there are receipts of cash into the business but the profit of the business is not affected.

Conversely, if a sole trader takes drawings out of the business or a company pays its shareholders a cash dividend then these are reductions in the cash balance of the business but do not reduce the profit level.

Purchase of non-current (fixed) assets

When non-current (fixed) assets are purchased by a business this will often mean a large payment of cash in order to acquire the asset. However, as you will have seen in your earlier accounting studies this does not directly affect the Income Statement (profit and loss account). The annual depreciation charge on the new asset is an expense rather than the full cash cost.

Sale of non-current (fixed) assets

When a non-current (fixed) asset is sold this will mean cash coming into the business, being the selling price of the asset. However, the profit of the business is only increased or decreased by any amount of profit or loss on the sale of this asset rather than the cash received.

Task 1

Which of the following transactions or events will affect profit in the same way as it affects the amount of cash in the business?

A   Purchase of a new computer for the business
B   Accrual of the electricity bill
C   Payment of the monthly wages at the end of the month
D   Sale of a company car

Cash and credit transactions

When we have talked about cash so far in this chapter we have generally meant the amount of money that the business has in its bank account. However we must be quite clear about the distinction between transactions which are for cash and those which are on credit.

A CASH TRANSACTION is one that takes place either with coins and notes, a cheque, a credit card or a debit card. Cash transactions are basically those for which money will be available in the business bank account almost immediately once the amounts have been paid into the bank.

A CREDIT TRANSACTION is one where the receipt or the payment is delayed for a period of time which is agreed between the two parties to the transaction. Many business sales and purchases are made on credit whereby the goods are delivered or received now but payment is agreed to be received or made in say 30 or 60 days time.

Task 2

In each of the following cases use the picklist to complete each sentence:

(a)   A cheque made out for £100 for the payment of rent is a [cash transaction/credit transaction]

(b)   Credit card sales of £800 are a [cash transaction/credit transaction]

(c)   Goods purchased for £250 with payment to be made on receipt of the invoice is a [cash transaction/credit transaction]

(d)   Goods and an invoice delivered to a customer today for payment in 30 days is a [cash transaction/credit transaction]

CALCULATING CASH FLOWS FROM FINANCIAL STATEMENT INFORMATION

For this Unit you will generally be required to prepare cash budgets from actual cash flow information. However, you also need to know how to calculate the value of cash transactions by adjusting the figures in an Income Statement (profit and loss account) and Statement of Financial Position (balance sheet) for the effects of accounting adjustments.

HOW IT WORKS

SC Fuel and Glass has a small lubricants division known as SCL. The budgeted Income Statement (profit and loss account) for the three months ending 31 December, is given below for SCL.

Budgeted Income Statement – three months ending 31 December

	£'000	£'000
Sales		840
Cost of sales		
Opening inventory (stock)	31	
Purchases	588	
	619	
Less: closing inventory (stock)	47	
		(572)
Gross profit		268
Operating expenses		(130)
Operating profit		138

The figure for operating expenses includes £24,000 of depreciation charges and an estimated profit of £3,000 on the sale of a non-current (fixed) asset that is expected to realise £20,000 during the period.

The budgeted Statements of Financial Position (balance sheets) for SCL at 30 September and 31 December are as follows:

Budgeted Statements of Financial Position

	31 December		30 September	
	£'000	£'000	£'000	£'000
Non-current (fixed) assets		948		809
Current assets				
Inventory (stock)	47		31	
Receivables (debtors)	50		62	
Prepayments for operating expenses	8		4	
	105		97	
Current liabilities				
Trade payables (creditors)	41		35	
Bank overdraft	3		–	
	44		35	
Net current assets		61		62
		1,009		871
Share capital		500		500
Retained earnings		509		371
		1,009		871

From the budgeted Income Statement (profit and loss account) and the budgeted Statements of Financial Position (balance sheets) we will now prepare the budgeted cash flows for sales, purchases and operating expenses.

Cash inflow from sales

The figure for sales is £840,000 however there were opening receivables (debtors) of £62,000 and closing receivables (debtors) of £50,000. This means that the actual cash flow from sales was £840,000 + £62,000 – £50,000 = £852,000. The reasoning for this is that the amount of sales actually made during the period were £840,000 but £50,000 had not paid at the end of the period but the opening receivables (debtors) of £62,000 would have paid.

Cash outflow for purchases

The figure for purchases in the Income Statement (profit and loss account) is £588,000 (note that we need the purchases figure not the cost of sales figure). Of these purchases £41,000 were not paid (being the closing payables (creditors) figure) whereas the opening payables (creditors) of £35,000 would have been paid. Therefore the cash flow for purchases for the period would be £588,000 + £35,000 – £41,000 = £582,000.

Depreciation

This is not a cash expense therefore there would be no cash flow for the period.

Sale of non-current (fixed) asset

The profit figure for the sale of the non-current (fixed) asset is not a cash flow, however, the anticipated sales proceeds of £20,000 are a budgeted cash inflow.

Cash payment for overheads

The charge for overheads in total is £130,000 but this includes a profit on sale of a non-current (fixed) asset of £3,000 and depreciation of £24,000. Therefore the cash based overheads are £130,000 - £24,000 + £3,000 = £109,000. However from the Statement of Financial Position (balance sheet) we can see that there are also opening prepayments of £4,000 and closing prepayments of £8,000. The opening prepayment figure of £4,000 has already been paid but the closing prepayment figure of £8,000 will be paid during the period. Therefore the estimated cash flow for overheads is £109,000 – £4,000 + £8,000 = £113,000.

Task 3

The Income Statement (profit and loss account) of a business for the three months ended 31 March shows that there are sales of £125,000, purchases of £80,000 and operating expenses of £15,000.

Extracts from the Statements of Financial Position (balance sheets) at 1 January and 31 March show the following:

	31 March	1 January
Receivables (debtors)	— £10,000	+£14,000
Trade payables (creditors)	— £11,000	+ £8,000
Accruals	— £2,000	+ £3,000

Calculate the actual cash flows for:

Sales	£ 129,000
Purchases	£ 77,000
Operating expenses	£ 16,000

Extracting capital expenditure figures

A Statement of Financial Position (balance sheet) will show the non-current (fixed) assets of a business at their carrying value which is normally their cost less accumulated depreciation. In the Income Statement (profit and loss account) the annual charge for depreciation will be shown. From this information it is possible to find the amount of capital expenditure incurred ie the amount of cash spent on non-current (fixed) assets in the period.

HOW IT WORKS

A business has an opening balance for non-current (fixed) assets in the Statement of Financial Position (balance sheet) of £100,000. The closing balance is £120,000. The Income Statement (profit loss account) shows that £10,000 of depreciation has been charged during the period.

The amount of cash spent on additional non-current (fixed) assets is:

	£
Opening balance	100,000
Less: depreciation charge	(10,000)
	90,000
Closing balance	120,000
Cash expenditure	30,000

The logic for this is that the balance for non-current (fixed) assets has increased by £20,000 on the Statement of Financial Position but this is after charging £10,000 of depreciation therefore in order to have increased this much there must have been £30,000 of new expenditure on non-current (fixed) assets.

CHAPTER OVERVIEW

- As a starting point for this Unit it is important to realise how vital cash is to a business even if the business is profitable as it must be able to meet its payments as and when they fall due.

- There are a number of differences between profit and cash due to the accruals concept, non-cash expenses, receipts or payments which do not affect profit, purchases and sales of non-current (fixed) assets.

- Cash transactions are where a form of money is received immediately whereas in a credit transaction goods are received or sent immediately but payment is delayed by agreement between the buyer and the seller.

- Budgeted Income Statement (profit and loss account) figures for sales, purchases, expenses etc can be used when combined with accounting adjustments such as accruals, prepayments and depreciation charges to find the budgeted cash flow figures for the period.

- Expenditure on non-current (fixed) assets may also need to be derived from the Statement of Financial Position (balance sheet) figures for non-current (fixed) assets and the depreciation charge in the Income Statement.

Keywords

Accruals concept – revenue and expenses are accounted for in the period in which they are incurred rather than the period in which the cash is received or paid

Non-cash expenses – expenses of the business which are charged to profit but do not affect the amount of cash in the business

Cash transaction – a transaction by cash, cheque, credit card or debit card

Credit transaction – a transaction where receipt or payment of cash is delayed for a period of time

Non-cash flows – charges or credits in the Income Statement (profit and loss account) which do not represent cash outflows or inflows

Working capital – inventories, receivables and payables

Cash flow from operating activities – the net cash flows caused by the operating activities of the business

TEST YOUR LEARNING

Test 1

Selecting from the picklists complete the following sentence:

Although it is important for a business to [make a profit/have a healthy cash balance] it can be argued that it is even more important for a business to [make a profit/have a healthy cash balance] in order to be able to pay amounts when they are due.

Test 2

Which of the following are factors that account for the difference between the amount of profit a business makes and its cash balance? Tick the relevant reasons.

Prepayment of rent	✓
Purchase of a non-current (fixed) asset	✓
Purchases of inventory for cash	
Depreciation	✓
Cash sales	

Test 3

Given below is the forecast Income Statement (profit and loss account) for a business for the three months ending 31 December together with forecast Statements of Financial Position (balance sheets) at 30 September and 31 December.

Forecast Income Statement for three months ending 31 December

	£'000	£'000
Sales		720
Opening inventory (stock)	78	
Purchases	471	
Less: closing inventory (stock)	(81)	
Cost of sales		(468)
Gross profit		252
Expenses		(130)
Operating profit		122

Included in the figure for expenses is £64,000 of depreciation charge for the year.

Forecast Statements of Financial Position

	31 December		30 September	
	£'000	£'000	£'000	£'000
Non-current (fixed) assets		584		426
Current assets				
Inventories (stock)	81		78	
Receivables (debtors)	75		60	
Cash	–		12	
	156		150	
Current liabilities				
Trade payables (creditors)	104		70	
Accruals	13		5	
	117		75	
Net current assets		39		75
		623		501
Share capital		400		400
Retained earnings		223		101
		623		501

From the forecast Income Statement (profit and loss account) and forecast Statements of Financial Position (balance sheets) calculate the cash flow figures for the three months ending 31 December.

	£'000
Sales receipts	705
Purchases payments	437
Expenses payments	58
Depreciation	0

2: Cash flow and profit

chapter 3:
CASH RECEIPTS AND PAYMENTS

chapter coverage 📖

Cash receipts and payments can be categorised in a number of ways according to their main characteristics and their differing patterns of cash flow. A cash budget needs to recognise different types of receipts and payments and incorporate a variety of payment patterns that arise both from the nature of the receipt or payment and from the effects of lagging. The topics that are covered are:

✍ Types of cash flows

✍ Sales receipts

✍ Payments for purchases

TYPES OF CASH FLOWS

Now that we have considered the importance of cash and the differences between cash and profit we must consider the different types of cash transactions or cash flows that a business will have.

Regular cash flows

The vast majority of the cash flows of a business will be REGULAR CASH FLOWS. This means that they will generally take place every week, every month, every quarter or annually. For example, if a business has weekly paid employees then they will be paid on Friday of every week. If a business has an agreement with its credit customers that goods are paid for at the end of the month after they are delivered then it will have receipts from customers at the end of each month. A business pays rent every quarter in advance so every three months there is a rental cash flow. Most companies pay their corporation tax liability for the year nine months after the year end so each year this payment will have to be made.

Irregular cash flows

Some cash flows of a business, however, are likely to be IRREGULAR CASH FLOWS. For example, the purchase of new non-current (fixed) assets is not necessarily something that is done every six months but as and when required.

Exceptional cash flows

Some of the cash flows of a business could also be regarded as EXCEPTIONAL CASH FLOWS or unpredictable cash flows. For example, if a machine breaks down then the costs of mending or replacing it would not have been predicted.

Variable and fixed cash flows

Some cash flows will be variable in amount although regular in time scale. For example, the amount of cash sales or receipts from customers is likely to vary each period. However, other cash flows are likely to be fixed in amount as well as regular. For example, the quarterly rent that a business pays for its building will be the same until there is a rent review and any amounts paid under a hire purchase agreement will be the same amount each period.

Capital and revenue receipts and payments

CAPITAL PAYMENTS are payments for the purchase of non-current (fixed) assets. They are assets that will be used within the business for a number of years. REVENUE PAYMENTS are payments concerned with the day to day running of the business. For example the purchase of a new company car will be a capital payment whereas the annual service of the car will be a revenue payment.

CAPITAL RECEIPTS are receipts from the owners of the business. For a sole trader or partnership this will be additional capital paid into the business by the owner or the partners. For a company this will be the issue of additional share capital. REVENUE RECEIPTS will be receipts relating to the day to day operations of the business such as sales receipts.

Types of cash receipt

Most cash receipts will be receipts from:

- Cash sales
- Credit sales
- Interest on money on deposit

All of these are fairly regular (though the amount in each time period may vary considerably). However other cash receipts might be irregular such as:

- Receipts of dividends from investments
- Additional capital raised
- Loan finance taken out
- Receipts from sale of non-current (fixed) assets

It is also possible that there may be exceptional receipts such as:

- Insurance monies received after theft of a company asset
- Receipt of a newly introduced government grant

Types of cash payment

Again, as with cash receipts, most cash payments are likely to be regular but there will tend to be a wider variety of payments than receipts. Regular cash payments (of varying amounts) might include:

- Cash payments for purchases
- Payments for purchases made on credit
- Payments of wages and salaries
- Payments for expenses
- Payments for VAT, PAYE and NIC
- Payments for corporation tax
- Interest payments on loans

Irregular payments might include:

- Drawings by a sole trader or partners in a partnership
- Dividends to shareholders in a company
- Payments to acquire new non-current (fixed) assets

Exceptional payments might include:

- Emergency expenses such as repair costs
- Bank charges on early withdrawal of funds

Different types of business

Different types of business will incur different types of cash flows. The structure of the business will initially affect the type of cash flows. For example, a company may make regular annual dividend payments to its shareholders whereas the amount and frequency of drawings that a sole trader takes out of the business will be their decision. A company will have to pay corporation tax on an annual basis whereas a sole trader pays income tax out of personal income rather than out of the business.

The trade of the business will also affect the type of cash flows that the business has. For example, a supermarket will have a large amount of cash sales and purchases on credit but little or no sales on credit. In contrast, a manufacturing business may make all of its sales on credit with no immediate receipts of cash for goods sold.

Service industries will tend to have large, monthly expenses for wages and salaries but only a few payments for purchases either on credit or for cash.

Format of a cash budget

All of these types of cash receipts and cash payments need to be incorporated in a cash budget. There is no set format for a cash budget and no regulations regarding how it should be set out but generally a cash budget will look something like this:

Cash budget for the quarter ending 31 December

	October	November	December
	£	£	£
Cash receipts			
Total receipts			
Cash payments			
Total payments			
Net cash flow for the month			
Opening balance			
Closing balance			

- Cash receipts will be analysed into their component parts and then totalled
- Cash payments will be analysed into their component parts and totalled
- Total receipts less total payments gives the net cash flow for the period
- The opening cash balance is then added in to give the closing cash balance

Task 1

Complete the table by picking the correct description to match the type of receipt or payment from the list below.

Type of receipt or payment	Description
Exceptional receipt	INSURANCE
Exceptional payment	HIRE

Sales on credit

Cash sales

Hire of machinery due to breakdown of own machine

Drawings

Dividend

Insurance claim receipt

Different types of information for a cash budget

When we considered the types of cash flows that a typical business might have, earlier in this chapter, we saw that these are many and varied. They include cash flows for sales, purchases, overheads or expenses, capital expenditure and receipts, and other payments and receipts such as additional capital and dividends or drawings.

As an accounting technician you will not necessarily have a detailed knowledge of all of these areas, therefore, you will require expert and detailed information from other personnel within the business in order to be able to prepare a cash budget. This information is likely to be reported in a variety of formats as different areas of the business will have differing reporting and accounting practices. In particular, you will typically need input from the following functions:

- Sales staff regarding the anticipated future levels of sales – this will probably be provided in terms of sales volumes and anticipated unit prices.

- Production staff regarding the expected levels of production and associated purchasing and other costs – purchases information is likely to be provided in terms of volumes whereas unit costs will most probably come from the accounting personnel

- Accounting personnel regarding prices, costs, wages, overheads etc

- Senior personnel regarding capital expenditure and sales, and plans for items such as the raising of additional capital or the payment of a dividend – this type of information is likely to come from minutes of directors' meetings where such matters will be discussed and determined.

Different types of cash flows

The format of a cash budget will depend upon the particular types of cash flow of that business. Equally, the preparation of a cash budget will depend upon the type of business. For a retail business the cash flows will involve the purchase of goods which are then resold either for cash or on credit. However, in a manufacturing business the materials required for production will have to be purchased and processed and then the finished goods will be sold. These different types of business will require different techniques in order to prepare the cash budget.

Preparation of a cash budget

The preparation of a cash budget, both in practice and in computer based tests, will require information from a variety of sources and this information must be brought together in order to determine the figures for each line of the cash budget.

We will start with one of the more complicated areas, which is determining the cash to be received from sales in each future period.

SALES RECEIPTS

Cash sales

Most businesses will have a mixture of cash sales and sales on credit. When preparing the cash budget the starting point will be the total expected sales for the period which will probably be provided by the sales department. A certain amount of these total sales, either reported as an absolute amount or as a percentage of total sales, will be cash sales which means that the cash inflow will take place at the same time as the sale.

Credit sales

When a business makes sales on credit this means that the cash for the sale will be received at some point in time after the sale. Typical examples of credit terms would be 30 days after the invoice date or 60 days after the invoice date. The receipt of money some time after the invoice date is known as a LAGGED RECEIPT.

Whatever credit terms are set for credit customers there will be some customers who do not adhere to them and will pay later than they are meant to. However, at this stage it is important to realise that some cash from credit sales will be received according to the stated credit terms but some will be received later. This means that of the credit sales in one particular month certain proportions of the cash will often be received in a number of different months after the sale.

HOW IT WORKS

The fuel division of SC Fuel and Glass is preparing its quarterly cash flow forecast for each of the three months of October, November and December.

The sales of the fuel division for these three months are expected to be as follows:

October	£680,000
November	£700,000
December	£750,000

Of these sales, 20% are cash sales and the remainder are sales on credit. Experience has shown that on average the customers for credit sales pay the monies due with the following pattern:

The month after sale	20%
Two months after sale	50%
Three months after sale	30%

Therefore, the cash for the October credit sales will be received in November, December and January. If we are preparing the cash flow forecast for the period from October to December then some of the cash inflows will be from credit sales in earlier periods therefore you will also require information about the credit sales for these earlier periods.

The total sales in July to September for the fuel division (again 20% of these were cash sales) are:

July	£600,000
August	£560,000
September	£620,000

We can now start to piece together the information required to prepare the cash from sales for October to December:

Cash budget – October to December

	October £	November £	December £
Cash receipts:			
Cash sales			
(20% of month sales)	136,000	140,000	150,000

Now we need to deal with sales on credit which are more complicated and will require a working:

WORKING – cash from credit sales

	October £	November £	December £
July sales			
(80% × 600,000 × 30%)	144,000		
August sales			
(80% × 560,000 × 50%)	224,000		
(80% × 560,000 × 30%)		134,400	
September sales			
(80% × 620,000 × 20%)	99,200		
(80% × 620,000 × 50%)		248,000	
(80% × 620,000 × 30%)			148,800
October sales			
(80% × 680,000 × 20%)		108,800	
(80% × 680,000 × 50%)			272,000
November sales			
(80% × 700,000 × 20%)			112,000
Cash from credit sales	467,200	491,200	532,800

Cash budget – October to December

	October £	November £	December £
Cash receipts:			
Cash sales	136,000	140,000	150,000
Cash from credit sales	467,200	491,200	532,800

Bad debts

When sales are made on credit there is always a possibility that some of the credit customers will never pay the amounts due. We will consider the effect this has on producing the cash flow forecast.

If it is considered that some invoices will never actually be paid by credit customers then these should be excluded from the cash receipts in the cash flow forecast. From experience most businesses will have an idea of the percentage of debts which tend to turn bad. As these are likely never to be received, they are not included as cash receipts.

HOW IT WORKS

The glass division of SC Fuel and Glass sells each sealed double-glazed unit for £80. All sales are on credit and the payment pattern from customers is estimated as follows:

- 30% pay in the month following the invoice

- The remainder pay two months after the invoice date but bad debts are generally about 5% of sales.

As bad debts will never turn into a cash inflow, the amount of cash received two months after the invoice date is 65% of the month's invoices rather than 70%.

Estimated sales for the glass division are:

	Units
August	10,200
September	12,000
October	13,200
November	14,100
December	14,800

Cash receipts from customers can then be calculated using a working.

WORKING – receipts from sales

	October £	November £	December £
August sales			
(10,200 × £80 × 65%)	530,400		
September sales			
(12,000 × £80 × 30%)	288,000		
(12,000 × £80 × 65%)		624,000	
October sales			
(13,200 × £80 × 30%)		316,800	
(13,200 × £80 × 65%)			686,400
November sales			
(14,100 × £80 × 30%)			338,400
Total receipts from sales	818,400	940,800	1,024,800

These figures can now be entered into the cash budget:

Cash budget – October to December

	October	November	December
	£	£	£
Cash receipts:			
Cash from credit sales	818,400	940,800	1,024,800

Task 2

A company makes credit sales with a typical payment pattern of 40% of the cash being received in the month after sale, 35% two months after the sale and 25% three months after the sale. Credit sales in August, September and October were £320,000, £360,000 and £400,000 respectively.

What are the cash receipts from credit sales received in November?

		£
August sales	320,000 × 25%	80,000
September sales	360,000 × 35%	126,000
October sales	400,000 × 40%	160,000
Total November receipts		366,000

PAYMENTS FOR PURCHASES

In a similar way to sales, purchases of the goods that a business buys can be made for cash or on credit. If the purchases are for cash then the cash outflow is at the same time as the purchase. However, if the purchase is made on credit then there will be a LAGGED PAYMENT where the cash is paid some time after the purchase is made. As with sales the business will have a typical payment pattern for its credit suppliers which can be used to find the cash outflow for each period.

Settlement discounts

When transactions are made on credit it is common practice for the seller to offer the buyer a SETTLEMENT DISCOUNT (or cash discount or prompt payment discount). This means that if the buyer pays within an agreed time period a certain percentage is deducted from the amount which is owed.

For cash budget purposes if a settlement discount is taken on purchases then this means that the cash payment will be earlier than normal but will be for the invoice amount less the settlement discount.

HOW IT WORKS

The purchasing manager for SC Fuel and Glass has provided you with the following information about the anticipated purchases of fuel for the fuel division for the period October to December.

October	£408,000
November	£420,000
December	£450,000

The accounts department provides you with the following information about the payment pattern for these purchases which are all made on credit terms.

- 25% of purchases are offered a 2% discount for payment in the month of the purchase and SC Fuels takes advantage of all such settlement discounts offered.

- 60% of purchases are paid in the month following the purchase

- 15% are paid two months after the date of purchase.

This means that 25% of purchases are paid in the month of purchase with 2% deducted. The remaining 75% of purchases are paid for in the following two months therefore we need information about the purchases in August and September in order to complete the cash flow forecast.

August purchases	£340,000
September purchases	£360,000

Again, we will need a working in order to determine the payments to suppliers in each of the three months.

WORKING – payments to credit suppliers

	October	November	December
	£	£	£
August purchases			
(340,000 × 15%)	51,000		
September purchases			
(360,000 × 60%)	216,000		
(360,000 × 15%)		54,000	
October purchases			
(408,000 × 25% × 98%)	99,960		
(408,000 × 60%)		244,800	
(408,000 × 15%)			61,200
November purchases			
(420,000 × 25% × 98%)		102,900	
(420,000 × 60%)			252,000
December purchases			
(450,000 × 25% × 98%)			110,250
Payments to credit suppliers	366,960	401,700	423,450

Settlement discounts offered on sales

In just the same way that settlement discounts can be taken on purchases a business may offer a settlement discount on its sales. This will affect the amount of cash inflow from sales on credit. Customers who take up the discount will pay earlier but will pay the invoice amount less the settlement discount.

If a settlement discount of 3% is offered on credit sales which are paid for in the month of sale then for those customers who take up the settlement discount the amount received will be just 97% of the invoiced amount.

3: Cash receipts and payments

Task 3

A business makes the following sales on credit:

August	£120,000
September	£100,000
October	£150,000

A settlement discount of 2.5% is offered for payment in the month of sale and this is taken up by 10% of customers. A further 50% of total customers pay one month after the sale and the remaining 40% of customers pay two months after the month of sale.

What is the cash inflow from credit customers for the month of October?

		£
August sales	120,000 × 40%	48,000
September sales	100,000 × 50%	50,000
October sales	150,000 × 10% × 97.5%	14,625
Total cash receipts		112,625

CHAPTER OVERVIEW

- Cash flows may be regular, irregular, exceptional, capital or revenue, variable or fixed.

- In order to prepare a cash budget, information will be required from many different sources within the organisation.

- When preparing a cash budget one of the most complicated areas is normally cash receipts from sales.

- Receipts from cash sales will take place at the same time as the sale but receipts from credit sales may be spread over a number of subsequent months.

- If bad debts are anticipated then these are amounts that will not be received in cash and are therefore excluded from the cash budget.

- Payments for purchases on credit will also typically be spread over a number of future months.

- If a settlement discount is offered on credit sales then the amount of anticipated cash inflow must be reduced and if settlement discounts are taken on purchases then the amount of the cash outflow must be reduced to reflect the smaller payment.

KEY WORDS

Regular cash flows – cash flows that take place on a regular basis be it daily, weekly, monthly, quarterly or annually

Irregular cash flows – cash flows which occur fairly infrequently and with no set pattern

Exceptional cash flows – unusual or unpredictable cash flows

Lagged receipt – receipt of cash which takes place some time after the related transaction

Lagged payment – payment of cash which takes place some time after the related transaction

Bad debts – invoiced amounts that it is considered will never be received in cash

Settlement discount – discount offered by the seller to the buyer in return for early payment of the amount due

TEST YOUR LEARNING

Test 1

A business has estimates of the following sales figures:

	£
October	790,000 ✗
November	750,000 ✓
December	720,000 ✓
January	700,000 ✓
February	730,000 ✓
March	760,000

Of these total sales figures 10% are likely to be cash sales and the remainder are credit sales. The payment pattern from customers in the past has been such that 40% of the total sales pay in the month after the sale and the remainder two months after the month of sale. However, of those that pay two months after the month of sale there are normally bad debts of 5% of sales.

Complete the table below to calculate the forecast cash receipts from sales for each of the months from January to March.

Forecast cash receipts

		January £	February £	March £
Cash sales		70.000	73,000	76,000
Credit sales		337.500		
		288.000	324,000	
			288,000	315.000
				292,000
Total receipts from sales		695.500	677,000	683,000

Test 2

A business has estimates of the following purchases figures:

	£
October	592,500 ✓
November	562,500 ✓
December	540,000 ✓
January	525,000 ✓
February	547,500 ✓
March	570,000

Purchases are all made on credit. 20% of purchases are offered a 2% discount for payment in the month after purchase and the business takes all such discounts. A further 65% of the purchases are paid for two months after the month of purchase and the remaining 15% are paid for three months after the date of purchase.

Complete the table below to calculate the cash payments for purchases for each of the months of January to March.

Forecast cash payments

		January	February	March
		£	£	£
October purchases		88.875		
November purchases		365.625	84375	
December purchases		105.840	351.000	81.000
January purchases			102.900	341.250
February purchases				107.310
Total payments for purchases		560.340	538.275	529.560

chapter 4:
FORECASTING FUTURE CASH RECEIPTS AND PAYMENTS

---

chapter coverage 📖

In the previous chapter we looked at the techniques required to prepare a forecast of receipts from sales and payments for purchases in preparation for producing a cash budget. In this chapter we consider in more depth how the figures that are included in the cash budget are estimated. We start with the use of time series analysis in the forecasting of future figures and then consider the effect of inflation on our forecasts.

The topics covered are:

✐ Time series analysis

✐ Graphical presentation

✐ Calculating a trend using moving averages

✐ Calculating seasonal variations

✐ Using time series analysis in cash budgeting

✐ Dealing with inflation in cash budgeting

✐ Using indices

TIME SERIES ANALYSIS

When preparing a cash budget an enormous number of figures must be estimated. These include:

- Sales figures
- Purchases figures
- Wages costs
- Overheads
- Exceptional receipts or payments.

One method of estimating sales and costs figures is to look at the past and determine any pattern there might be in these figures over time in order to estimate the likely future figures. One method of analysing past or historic figures is to use the technique of TIME SERIES ANALYSIS.

Time series

A TIME SERIES is simply a record of figures that have occurred over a past period of time. For example each of the following would be an example of a time series:

- Daily takings for the last three months
- Weekly labour costs for the last six months
- Monthly sales for the last three years
- Quarterly sales quantities for the last five years
- Annual number of employees for the last fifteen years

Using time series

The figures in a time series can be analysed in a variety of ways in order to produce results that can be used within budgeting. One method of presenting the time series information is to produce a graph with time plotted along the horizontal axis and the figures on the vertical axis. This can give a useful visual presentation of the figures over the time period.

HOW IT WORKS

At the end of December 20X8 the management accountant of SC Fuel and Glass decided to carry out a time series analysis on the monthly sales of the fuel division for the last year. The sales figures for each of those months are given below.

	Sales £'000
Time period	
January	2,030
February	1,570
March	1,620
April	2,100
May	2,080
June	1,740
July	1,690
August	2,190
September	2,150
October	1,830
November	1,780
December	2,200

From these figures we can see that the fuel business is clearly seasonal with higher sales in some months of the year than in other months. However these highs and lows can be more easily seen when illustrated on a graph.

SC Fuel and Glass – Fuel division – monthly sales

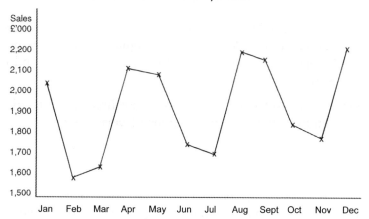

From the graph we can quite easily see that even though the sales do vary each month due to the seasonality of the business there is a definite upwards movement of the figures over time or trend.

THE TREND

The TREND of a series of figures in a time series is the way in which the figures are moving in general despite various fluctuations caused by seasonality. One very simple way of determining the trend is to draw a line of best fit on a time series graph which shows in general how the figures are changing.

HOW IT WORKS

Returning to the fuel division sales a TREND LINE could be drawn onto the graph as follows:

SC Fuel and Glass – Fuel division – monthly sales

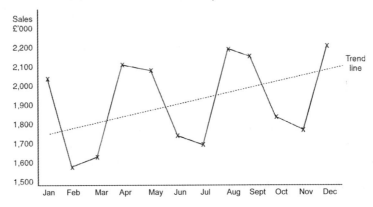

This line now gives a graphical presentation of the trend in sales for the fuel division. If the trend in future sales were to be estimated from this graph then the line would be extended into, say the first four months of 20X9, and the trend figure for sales read off the graph.

However, there are more technical methods of determining the trend of a time series and one of these is the technique of using moving averages.

Moving averages

A moving average is the average of each successive group of figures from the time series. A moving average can be taken using either an even or an odd number of figures for each average. For this syllabus, however, the calculations will be based upon odd numbers which is slightly easier.

HOW IT WORKS

We return to the sales figures for the fuel division for the last year.

	Sales £'000
Time period	
January	2,030
February	1,570
March	1,620
April	2,100
May	2,080
June	1,740
July	1,690
August	2,190
September	2,150
October	1,830
November	1,780
December	2,200

We have already seen from the graph that there is a general upwards trend in the figures but distinct seasonal variations. In time series analysis we attempt to first calculate the trend of the figures using moving averages and then to identify these SEASONAL VARIATIONS.

We will start by calculating a three-period moving average for the sales figures. We begin with calculating the average of the first three months, January to March:

$$\frac{2,030 + 1,570 + 1,620}{3} = 1,740$$

We then move onto the next group of three months, February to April:

$$\frac{1,570 + 1,620 + 2,100}{3} = 1,763$$

and so on ......

Each of these average figures is shown in the table against the middle month for each calculation – therefore the first average of 1,740 is shown against February, the next one against March and so on.

	Sales £'000	Moving average £'000
Time period		
January	2,030	
February	1,570	1,740
March	1,620	1,763
April	2,100	1,933
May	2,080	1,973
June	1,740	1,837
July	1,690	1,873
August	2,190	2,010
September	2,150	2,057
October	1,830	1,920
November	1,780	1,937
December	2,200	

The moving average figures show a clear increase and indicate the trend of the figures.

We can now see that the trend for the sales figures shows an average increase in each month of about £22,000 ((1,937 – 1,740)/9 changes in trend).

Task 1

Given below are the monthly costs incurred by a factory.

Complete the table below to calculate the monthly sales volume trend using a three month moving average.

	Monthly costs £'000	3 month moving average £'000
January	129	
February	138	134
March	135	138
April	142	142
May	150	148
June	153	150
July	148	151
August	151	154
September	162	159
October	165	166
November	172	167
December	164	

SEASONAL VARIATIONS

Each figure in the original time series can be said to be made up of a number of different elements. Technically these are:

- Trend
- Cyclical variation
- Seasonal variation
- Random variation

We have already seen that the trend is the general movement of the time series calculated using moving averages. The CYCLICAL VARIATION is the long-term variations due to general economic conditions. Such variations typically take place over a period of about seven years and therefore for most practical purposes are ignored when dealing with time series analysis.

The RANDOM VARIATION is variations in the figures due to unexplained or random events. Again, by their very nature, they tend to be ignored for time series analysis.

Therefore we are left with the trend and the seasonal variation. The TREND is the general long-term movement of the time series and the SEASONAL VARIATION is the effect on the actual figure of that particular season. There are two models which are used in time series analysis – the additive model and the multiplicative model.

Additive model

The ADDITIVE MODEL is where each actual figure in the time series is made up as follows:

$$A = T + S$$

Where: A   =   Actual figure

          T   =   Trend figure

          S   =   Seasonal variation

Therefore the seasonal variation is calculated as:

$$S = A - T$$

Multiplicative model

The MULTIPLICATIVE MODEL is where each actual figure in the time series is made up as follows:

$$A = T \times S$$

Where: A = Actual figure
  T = Trend figure
  S = Seasonal variation

Therefore the seasonal variation is calculated as:

$$S = \frac{A}{T}$$

For this syllabus the calculation of seasonal variations is not required but you do need to appreciate that moving averages can be used to identify expected seasonal variations.

USING TIME SERIES ANALYSIS IN CASH BUDGETING

In the previous sections we looked at how to calculate a trend using moving averages. Now we will consider how this information can be used in the cash budgeting process.

Time series analysis in budgeting is used in order to estimate future figures based upon the past trend and seasonal variations that have been calculated. This process of using the historical information to estimate future figures is known as EXTRAPOLATION.

HOW IT WORKS

The management accountant at SC Fuel and Glass, having carried out the time series analysis on the fuel division sales, decides to use the information to estimate the sales figures for each of the first four months of 20X9.

The last trend figure that was calculated was for November 20X8 at a figure of £1,937,000. We have already seen that on average the trend is increasing by £22,000 each month therefore we can use this information to calculate the trend figure for each of the first four months of 20X9. The figure for January 20X9 is calculated as the last trend figure of £1,937,000 plus two additions of £22,000 to cover December 20X8 as well as January 20X9 and so on.

		Trend £'000
20X9	January (1,937 + (2 × 22))	1,981
	February (1,981 + 22)	2,003
	March (2,003 + 22)	2,025
	April (2,025 + 22)	2,047

We now have to take into account the seasonal variations. Under the additive model each seasonal variation is either added to, or deducted from, the trend to determine the estimated future sales. The seasonal variation in each case is given below in order to adjust the trend and estimate the future sales figure.

Seasonal variation – additive model

	January £'000	February £'000	March £'000	April £'000
Seasonal variation	+ 174	– 170	– 235	+ 231

		Trend £'000	Seasonal variation £'000	Estimated sales £'000
20X9	January (1,937 + (2 × 22))	1,981	+ 174	2,155
	February (1,981 + 22)	2,003	– 170	1,833
	March (2,003 + 22)	2,025	– 235	1,790
	April (2,025 + 22)	2,047	+ 231	2,278

Under the multiplicative model the trend is multiplied by the seasonal variation percentage in order to estimate the future sales for each month.

Seasonal variation – multiplicative model

	January	February	March	April
Seasonal variation	109.0%	91.3%	87.6%	112.1%

		Trend £'000	Seasonal variation %	Estimated sales £'000
20X9	January	1,981	109.0	2,159
	February	2,003	91.3	1,829
	March	2,025	87.6	1,774
	April	2,047	112.1	2,295

Problems with using time series analysis for forecasting

Time series analysis can be a useful method of attempting to forecast future sales and cost figures. However you should also be aware that the technique does have its limitations:

- The less historic data available the less reliable the results will be

- The further into the future we forecast the less reliable the results will be

- There is an assumption that the trend and seasonal variations from the past will continue into the future

- Cyclical and random variations have been ignored.

Task 2

The trend figures for a business's quarterly sales are given below together with the seasonal variations using the additive model.

			£'000
20X6	Q2		319
	Q3		344
	Q4		354
20X7	Q1		346
	Q2		342
	Q3		362
	Q4		365
20X8	Q1		352
	Q2		348
	Q3		369

The seasonal variations have been calculated as follows:

Q1 −21.3

Q2 −27.6

Q3 +14.1

Q4 +34.8

The average quarterly sales trend increase is £'000 **5.6**

Use this information to determine the estimated sales figures for the first four quarters of 20X9.

20X9	Forecast trend	Seasonal variation	Forecast sales
	£'000	£'000	£'000
Q1	380.2	−21.3	358.9
Q2	385.8	−27.6	358.2
Q3	391.4	+14.1	405.5
Q4	397	+34.8	431.8

INFLATION AND CASH BUDGETS

INFLATION is the increase in prices of goods and services over a period of time. If we are trying to estimate future figures for cash receipts from sales or cash payments for goods or expenses then any increases caused by inflation must be taken into consideration.

Specific increases

In most economies there will be inflation to some degree and this is often dealt with by a one-off increase in sales price or, for example, an annual increase in the hourly rate paid to the workforce. Such anticipated increases should be built into the cash budget.

HOW IT WORKS

The glass division of SC Fuel and Glass is preparing its cash budget for the three months ended 31 March 20X9. The selling price of the sealed double-glazed units has been £80 per unit for more than a year and it has been decided to increase this price by 10% per unit from 1 March 20X9.

The workforce is currently paid at a rate of £8 per hour and each double-glazed unit requires 1.5 hours of labour. From 1 February there is to be a 7.5% increase in the hourly wage rate.

Sales and production for the three months of January to March 20X9 are estimated as follows:

	Sales	Production
	Units	Units
January	13,800	13,400
February	13,500	13,600
March	13,900	14,000

The figures that will be used in the cash budget for sales and for wages costs will need to incorporate the planned increases in prices.

Sales

	£
January (13,800 × £80)	1,104,000
February (13,500 × £80)	1,080,000
March (13,900 × (£80 × 1.10))	1,223,200

Wages

	£
January (13,400 × 1.5 × £8)	160,800
February (13,600 × 1.5 x (£8 × 1.075))	175,440
March (14,000 × 1.5 × (£8 × 1.075))	180,600

Task 3

A business currently sells its single product for a price of £95 per unit. However from 1 November 20X9 this price is to be increased by 5%. Sales quantities are anticipated to be 43,000 units in October and 40,000 in November.

Complete the table below to calculate the expected valued of the business's sales in October and November.

	Expected sales value £
October	4,085.000
November	3.990,000

General price increases

In some cases, particularly when considering expenses, there may not be any known specific increases in prices, however experience has shown that expenses tend to increase on average at a particular level which may well be in line with the general level of inflation within the economy. Again, such general expectations of increased prices should be built into the cash budget.

HOW IT WORKS

The fuel division of SC Fuel and Glass is also preparing its cash budget for the quarter ending 31 March 20X9. In December 20X8 the overheads were estimated to be £87,000 which included £12,000 of depreciation charges. It is now considered that these overheads, excluding depreciation, will increase by 0.5% each month.

The figures to be included in the cash budget for overheads will therefore be as follows:

	£
January (75,000 × 1.005)	75,375
February (75,375 × 1.005)	75,752
March (75,752 × 1.005)	76,131

Task 4

A business purchases raw materials at a current cost, September 20X9, of £15.80 per kg. It purchases 100,000 kgs each month and it is anticipated that the price will rise by 1.2% each month.

Complete the table below to calculate the expected value of purchases in October and November 20X9.

	Expected purchases value £
October	1,598,960
November	1,618,148

INDICES

One common method of expressing changes in prices is by the use of indices. An INDEX is a measure of the changes over time in the price of an item or a group of items. Index numbers are normally expressed in terms of a BASE YEAR or BASE PERIOD for which the value assigned to the index is 100. Any subsequent increases or decreases in the price of the item are then reflected in the value of the index.

Calculation of an index

The first step in the calculation of an index is to determine the base year and set the price in that year at a value of 100. The price in subsequent years is then expressed as a proportion of 100. If the price is higher than the base year price the index will be greater than 100 but if it is lower than the base year price the index will be less than 100.

HOW IT WORKS

The glass division of SC Fuel and Glass has seen the price of glass sheets vary over the past few years. The average price for glass sheets for the past six years has been as follows:

20X3	£14.60
20X4	£14.40
20X5	£15.20
20X6	£15.00
20X7	£15.60
20X8	£16.00

Using 20X3 as the base year an index for these prices can be constructed.

		Index value
20X3		100.0
20X4	14.40/14.60 × 100	98.6
20X5	15.20/14.60 × 100	104.1
20X6	15.00/14.60 × 100	102.7
20X7	15.60/14.60 × 100	106.8
20X8	16.00/14.60 × 100	109.6

Using indices in cash budgeting

In some instances, when preparing a cash budget, you may not know the precise future price of either sales that are to be made or purchases or expenses that are to be paid for. However, you may be given a price index for the item and an anticipated value for that index in the future and this can be used to determine the value of the anticipated cash inflow or cash outflow.

Specific and general price indices

A SPECIFIC PRICE INDEX is an index which relates to a specific item such as the goods that a business purchases or the items that it sells. A GENERAL PRICE INDEX is an index which measures the price of a variety of goods and services and is, in effect, a measure of general inflation.

Retail Price Index

The best known general price index in the UK is the RETAIL PRICE INDEX (RPI) which measures changes in the cost of items of expenditure in the average household and therefore provides a good indication of the general level of inflation in the economy. The RPI is based upon a base month of January 1987 when the index was set at 100. By May 2010 the index was at the level of 223.6.

HOW IT WORKS

Returning to SC Fuel and Glass, the sales for the fuel division were £750,000 in December 20X8. This was when the specific price index for fuel stood at 187.4. The quantity of fuel to be sold in January 20X9 and February 20X9 is considered to be similar to that in December 20X8 but the price index is expected to be 190.1 in January 20X9 and 192.3 in February 20X9.

From this information we can forecast the expected sales value of fuel in January and February.

		£
January	£750,000 × 190.1/187.4	760,806
February	£750,000 × 192.3/187.4	769,610

The general overheads of the fuel division (excluding depreciation) in December were £75,000. It is now believed that overheads increase in line with the general inflation rate as indicated by the RPI. In December 20X8 the RPI is 196.6. It is anticipated that the RPI will be 197.2 in January 20X9 and 198.1 in February 20X9. Using this information we can determine the estimated overheads figure (excluding depreciation) for each of the two months.

		£
January	£75,000 × 197.2/196.6	75,229
February	£75,000 × 198.1/196.6	75,572

Task 5

A business believes that its general overheads increase in line with the Retail Price Index. In April 20X9 the general overheads were £200,000 and the RPI was 195.3. The RPI is anticipated to be 195.9 in May 20X9 and 196.4 in June 20X9.

What is the expected general overhead cost in June 20X9?

A £201,126

B £392,800

C £200,614

D £198,880

CHAPTER OVERVIEW

- Cash budgets are based upon estimates of future cash inflows and outflows. One method of estimating future figures such as sales or costs is to use time series analysis.

- A time series is a series of historical figures over a period of time and the first stage is to determine the trend of these figures using moving averages.

- Once the trend has been determined the seasonal variations can be calculated either using the additive model or the multiplicative model.

- Once the trend and any seasonal variations are known then this information can be used to estimate future figures by extrapolating the trend line into the future and applying the appropriate seasonal variation.

- In estimating future cash flows account must be taken of any anticipated inflation. This may be in the form of a one-off price increase or a more general period by period increase.

- One method of expressing a change in prices is using an index. This could be a specific price index for a particular item of goods or services or a general price index such as the Retail Price Index (RPI).

- An index, with its associated future estimated value, can be used to convert a current cash flow value to its estimated actual future value.

KEY WORDS

Time series analysis – a method of analysing historic data in order to use the results for future calculations

Time series – any record of figures occurring over a past period

Trend – the general movement in a time series over time

Trend line – a line drawn onto a graph of a time series to indicate the general movements of the figures

Seasonal variations – variations of the figures for particular time periods from the trend due to seasonal factors

Cyclical variations – long-term movements in a time series due to general economic conditions

Random variations – variations in time series figures due to random or unexplained events

Additive model – a time series model where the actual figure is made up of the trend plus the seasonal variation

Multiplicative model – a time series model where the actual figure is made up of the trend multiplied by the seasonal variation

Extrapolation – using historic data to make estimates of future figures

Inflation – the increase in prices of goods and services over time

Index – a measure of changes in price over time

Base year/period – the year or period upon which an index is based and to which the index value of 100 is assigned

Specific price index – a price index relating to a specific item of goods or services

General price index – a price index relating to a variety of goods and services

Retail Price Index – a general index which measures changes in the cost of items of expenditure in the average household

TEST YOUR LEARNING

Test 1

Given below are the daily takings in a restaurant that is open five days a week, Tuesday to Saturday.

	Tues	Wed	Thurs	Fri	Sat
	£	£	£	£	£
Week 1	560	600	630	880	930
Week 2	540	590	640	850	940
Week 3	550	560	600	870	970

Complete the table below to calculate the 5 day moving average of the daily takings.

		Takings	5 day moving average
		£	£
Week 1	Tuesday	560	
	Wednesday	600	
	Thursday	630	720
	Friday	880	716
	Saturday	930	714
Week 2	Tuesday	540	716
	Wednesday	590	710
	Thursday	640	712
	Friday	850	714
	Saturday	940	708
Week 3	Tuesday	550	700
	Wednesday	560	704
	Thursday	600	710
	Friday	870	
	Saturday	970	

Test 2

Given below are the units produced in a factory from Monday to Friday for each day for three weeks.

	Mon	Tues	Wed	Thurs	Fri
	Units	Units	Units	Units	Units
Week 1	1,400	1,600	1,800	1,800	1,550
Week 2	1,380	1,620	1,830	1,810	1,500
Week 3	1,450	1,650	1,850	1,840	1,570

(a) **Complete the table below to calculate the trend of these figures using a 5 day moving average.**

		Production in units	Trend in units
Week 1	Monday	1400	
	Tuesday	1600	
	Wednesday	1800	1630
	Thursday	1800	1626
	Friday	1550	1630
Week 2	Monday	1380	1636
	Tuesday	1620	1638
	Wednesday	1830	1628
	Thursday	1810	1642
	Friday	1500	1648
Week 3	Monday	1450	1652
	Tuesday	1650	1658
	Wednesday	1850	1672
	Thursday	1840	
	Friday	1570	

(b) **Calculate the average increase in the trend over the period.**

4.2

(c) The daily seasonal variations for this time series using the multiplicative model have been calculated as follows:

Mon	Tues	Wed	Thur	Fri
86.1%	99.2%	111.1%	110.5%	93.1%

Using the trend and the seasonal variations complete the table below to forecast the production volume for the following week.

Day	Trend in units	Seasonal variation	Forecast volume in units
Monday	1684.6	86.1%	1450
Tuesday	1688.8	99.2%	1675
Wednesday	1693	111.1%	1880
Thursday	1697.2	110.5%	1875
Friday	1701.4	93.1%	1584

Test 3

It is December 20X8 and a business is preparing its cash budget for the first quarter of 20X9. The following sales and purchases figures have been produced:

	Sales	Purchases
	Units	Units
January	5,000	5,200
February	5,600	5,800
March	5,700	5,500

The current cost of purchases is £20 per unit and these are sold for £35 per unit. The business has been informed by its supplier that purchase prices will be increased from 1 February 20X9 by 5% and the business has decided to increase its selling price by 8% from 1 January 20X9.

Purchases are all paid for in the month of purchase but the cash receipts from sales all occur in the month following the sale. Sales in December 20X8 were 4,800 units.

Use the table below to calculate the estimated cash inflows from sales and cash payments for purchases for January to March 20X9.

	Sales in units	Price per unit	Cash inflow	Purchases in units	Price per unit	Cash outflow
		£	£		£	£
Jan	4800	35	168.000	5200	20	104.000
Feb	5600	37.8	189.000	5800	21	121800
Mar	5600	37.8	211680	5500	21	115500

Test 4

A business has general overheads of £160,000 in September 20X9 but it is anticipated that these will increase by 1.75% per month for the next few months. Overheads are paid the month after they are incurred.

What is the cash outflow for overheads for the month of December 20X9?

A   £162,800

B   £165,600

Ⓒ   £168,548

D   £165,649

Test 5

A business makes purchases of a particular raw material which has a cost of £10.80 per kg in September 20X9. The actual and estimated specific price index for this material is as follows:

	Price index
September 20X9 (actual)	148.5
October 20X9 (estimate)	151.6
November 20X9 (estimate)	154.2
December 20X9 (estimate)	158.7

Complete the table below to calculate the expected price per kg (to the nearest penny) of the raw material in each of the months from October to December.

	Index calculation	Expected price £
October	10.80/148.5 × 151.6	11.03
November	10.80/148.5× 154.2	11.21
December	10.80/148.5 × 158.7	11.54

chapter 5:
PREPARING CASH BUDGETS

chapter coverage 📖

This chapter will bring together much of the information studied in the previous chapters in the form of the preparation of the cash budget. Cash budgets provide decision-makers with an effective tool for cash management which will be considered in the final chapters of this Text.

The topics covered are:

✍   Format for cash budgets

✍   Other cash payments and receipts

✍   Bank interest paid or received

✍   Manufacturing organisations

FORMAT FOR CASH BUDGETS

There is no set or statutory format for cash budgets but as an important management tool they should be set out in a manner which is useful to management decision-makers. This may differ from business to business but in general terms the following information will be shown:

- Analysis of the sources of cash receipts and the total of cash receipts for the period
- Analysis of the sources of cash payments and the total of cash payments for the period
- Net cash flow for the period
- Bank balance brought forward
- Bank balance carried forward

Preparation of a cash budget

The preparation of a cash budget, both in practice and in computer based tests, will require information from a variety of sources and this information must be incorporated in order to determine the figures for each line of the cash budget.

In Chapter 3 of this Text we looked in detail at the figures for cash receipts from sales including credit sales, the effect of lagging, settlement discounts and bad debts. We also considered cash payments for purchases including credit purchases, the effects of lagging and settlement discounts.

In this chapter we will consider the further elements of cash flow in order to prepare a full cash budget.

OTHER CASH PAYMENTS AND RECEIPTS

In most cash budget calculations the determination of the amount of cash receipts from sales and cash payments for purchases are the hardest elements to deal with. However there will be a number of other types of cash payments and cash receipts that will need to be considered and included in the cash budget.

Wages and salaries

In almost all cases net wages and salaries tend to be paid in the month in which they are incurred and therefore there is no difficulty with either calculation or timing of the cash flows.

Overheads

Expenses or overheads will normally be paid in the month in which they are incurred, however, care should be taken in a computer based test to read the information given as some may be lagged payments.

Care should also be taken with depreciation which is not a cash cost. Often the figure for overheads will include an amount which represents depreciation for the period and this must be excluded in order to find the cash payment.

Irregular or exceptional payments

Other types of payments that are not incurred on a regular basis may be included in the information regarding cash payments. These may include:

- VAT payments (usually quarterly)
- Payment details for the acquisition of non-current (fixed) assets
- Dividend payments
- Loan repayments

In a computer based test details of the precise timing of these payments will be given to you.

Irregular or exceptional receipts

Again, detailed information about such receipts will be given in a computer based test. The most common type of irregular receipts are cash received from the sale of non-current (fixed) assets. These are sometimes lagged receipts if the sale is made on credit and the cash is therefore received some time after the sale.

Another possible type of irregular receipt might be the receipt of additional capital. For a sole trader or a partnership this will be additional money paid into the business by the owner or partners. For a company this will be the proceeds from an issue of additional share capital. For a sole trader, partnership or company there might also be a cash receipt from further loan capital being taken out.

HOW IT WORKS

Having dealt with the cash receipts from sales and the cash payments for purchases for the fuel division of SC Fuel and Glass in Chapter 3 we will now complete the cash budget using the following additional information:

- Gross wages and salaries are £113,000 each month, payable at the end of the month in which they are incurred

- 75% of general overheads are paid in the month in which they are incurred with the remainder being paid in the following month. General overheads were £80,000 in September and October rising to £87,000 in November and December

- Included in the general overheads figures is a monthly amount of £12,000 for depreciation of non-current (fixed) assets

- In January the fuel division is having a new property constructed and in December a down-payment of £120,000 is required to be paid to the building company

- In October the quarterly VAT payment of £45,000 is to be paid

- In October a non-current (fixed) asset is to be sold for £18,000 but it was agreed that the asset would be paid for in two equal instalments in November and December

- The cash balance at the end of September was an overdraft balance of £29,500.

The receipts from sales and the payments for purchases that were calculated in Chapter 3 are as follows:

Cash budget – October to December

	October	November	December
	£	£	£
Cash receipts:			
Cash sales	136,000	140,000	150,000
Cash from credit sales	467,200	491,200	532,800
Cash payments:			
Payments for credit purchases	366,960	401,700	423,450

You are now to complete the cash budget for the fuel division for the three months ended 31 December.

- Wages and salaries are a straightforward cash payment in the month incurred

- For the general overheads, first, the depreciation charge must be removed as this is a non-cash expense and then a working will be required to ensure that the correct amount of cash payment is shown in each month as 25% of the overheads are paid in the month after they are incurred.

WORKING – General overheads

	October	November	December
	£	£	£
September overheads			
(25% × (80,000 – 12,000))	17,000		
October overheads			
(75% × (80,000 – 12,000))	51,000		
(25% × (80,000 – 12,000))		17,000	
November overheads			
(75% × (87,000 – 12,000))		56,250	
(25% × (87,000 – 12,000))			18,750
December overheads			
(75% × (87,000 – 12,000))			56,250
Total overhead payment	68,000	73,250	75,000

- The construction down-payment is a straightforward December cash flow
- The VAT is a cash payment in October
- The non-current (fixed) asset sale cash receipt will be £9,000 in the months of November and December
- Using the opening cash balance at 1 October, the opening and closing balances each month can be calculated

Cash budget – October to December

	October	November	December
	£	£	£
Cash receipts:			
Cash sales	136,000	140,000	150,000
Cash from credit sales	467,200	491,200	532,800
Sale of non-current (fixed) asset		9,000	9,000
Total cash receipts	603,200	640,200	691,800
Cash payments:			
Payments for credit purchases	366,960	401,700	423,450
Wages and salaries	113,000	113,000	113,000
General overheads	68,000	73,250	75,000
Capital expenditure			120,000
VAT	45,000		
Total cash payments	592,960	587,950	731,450
Net cash flow for the month	10,240	52,250	(39,650)
Opening cash balance	(29,500)	(19,260)	32,990
Closing cash balance	(19,260)	32,990	(6,660)

Note that the closing cash balance at the end of each period is the opening cash balance at the start of the next period.

Task 1

A company is preparing its cash flow forecast for the month of November. The estimated cash sales in November are £64,000 and sales on credit in October and November are estimated to be £216,000 and £238,000. It is estimated that 40% of credit customers pay in the month of sale after deducting a 2% discount and the remainder pay one month after the date of sale.

Purchases are all on credit payable in the month following the purchase. Purchases were £144,000 in October and £165,000 in November.

Wages and salaries of £80,000 a month are payable in the month in which they are incurred as are general overheads of £65,000. The general overheads figure includes a depreciation charge of £15,000 each month. A dividend of £20,000 is to be paid to the shareholders in November.

The balance on the cash account at the beginning of November is anticipated to be an overdraft balance of £10,200.

Prepare the cash budget for the month of November. Cash inflows should be entered as positive figures and cash outflows as negative figures.

Cash budget – November

	£
Cash receipts:	
Cash sales	64000
Credit sales	222 896
Total cash receipts	286 896
Cash payments:	
Purchases on credit	144.000
Wages and salaries	80.000
Overheads	50.000
Dividend	20000
Total cash payments	294000
Net cash flow	(7104)
Opening balance	(10 200)
Closing balance	(17304)

BANK INTEREST PAID OR RECEIVED

If the business has a bank overdraft then it can expect to be paying interest on that overdraft. Conversely, if the bank account is in credit then the business may be receiving interest from the bank.

Therefore a further adjustment might be required to a cash budget if it is anticipated that the cash balance during the period will be an overdraft balance for interest paid or if the bank balance is expected to be in credit for interest received.

If there is an overdraft balance then the bank will charge interest on the amount of the overdraft. This interest will be a cash outflow based upon the overdraft amount, which will normally be paid in the following month. If the bank account is in credit and interest is receivable from the bank then this will be a cash inflow which will normally be received in the following month.

HOW IT WORKS

We will return to the cash budget for the fuel division of SC Fuel and Glass.

The cash budget to date appears as follows:

Cash budget – October to December

	October £	November £	December £
Cash receipts:			
Cash sales	136,000	140,000	150,000
Cash from credit sales	467,200	491,200	532,800
Sale of non-current (fixed) asset		9,000	9,000
Total cash receipts	603,200	640,200	691,800
Cash payments:			
Payments for credit purchases	366,960	401,700	423,450
Wages and salaries	113,000	113,000	113,000
General overheads	68,000	73,250	75,000
Capital expenditure			120,000
VAT	45,000		
Total cash payments	592,960	587,950	731,450
Net cash flow for the month	10,240	52,250	(39,650)
Opening cash balance	(29,500)	(19,260)	32,990
Closing cash balance	(19,260)	32,990	(6,660)

129600

At the end of September there is an overdraft balance of £29,500 and at the end of October an overdraft balance of £19,260. Say that interest is charged at 1% per month on these balances in the following month. Therefore a further cash outflow line must be included for overdraft interest based upon the balance at the end of the previous month. This in turn will have an effect on the net cash flow for the month and the overdraft balance at the end of October.

The overdraft interest cash payment in October will be based upon the overdraft balance at 1 October:

$$1\% \times £29,500 = £295$$

This is entered as a cash outflow which in turn means that the overdraft balance at the end of October will increase to £19,555. Therefore the overdraft interest in November will be:

$$1\% \times £19,555 = £196$$

Cash budget – October to December

	October £	November £	December £
Cash receipts:			
Cash sales	136,000	140,000	150,000
Cash from credit sales	467,200	491,200	532,800
Sale of non-current (fixed) assets		9,000	9,000
Total cash receipts	603,200	640,200	691,800
Cash payments:			
Payments for credit purchases	366,960	401,700	423,450
Wages and salaries	113,000	113,000	113,000
General overheads	68,000	73,250	75,000
Capital expenditure			120,000
VAT	45,000		
Overdraft interest	295	196	
Total cash payments	593,255	588,146	731,450
Net cash flow for the month	9,945	52,054	(39,650)
Opening cash balance	(29,500)	(19,555)	32,499
Closing cash balance	(19,555)	32,499	(7,151)

Note that the introduction of the overdraft interest has affected each of the month-end balances.

If you are told that interest is receivable on credit balances then the procedure is the same as for overdraft interest but is a cash inflow:

- Calculate the interest based upon the balance at the start of the period
- Include as a cash inflow in the following month

Revised cash budgets

As we have seen cash budgets are prepared using many forecasting techniques and assumptions. There will be occasions both in practice and in computer based tests when there will be changes from the original assumptions which will require changes in the cash budget. The types of changes that may need to be incorporated into a cash budget include the following:

- Changes in volumes – if there are adjustments to anticipated sales volumes in units then this will affect the cash receipts figures as there will be different amounts for cash and/or credit sales. There may also be changes in purchases volumes in units which will also affect the cash payment figures for purchases.

- Changes in prices – the original cash budget will have been based on assumptions about selling prices per unit and purchase prices per unit. In turn these may have been based upon assumptions regarding specific or general price increases (see Chapter 4). If there are changes in the selling price per unit then this will affect the figures for cash receipts. If there are changes in the purchase price per unit then this will affect the figures for cash payments.

- Changes in payment patterns – this might include situations where it is decided that either the payment pattern for sales to customers or purchases from suppliers are not as they were originally determined. For example it might be felt that credit customers are taking longer periods of credit than was originally assumed. Although this will not affect the amount of credit sales it will affect the period in which the cash is received. Similarly various purchases and expenses may remain at the same amount but in a different time period. For example it may have been originally assumed that the purchase of a new non-current (fixed) asset would be paid for in full in cash in March. However the business has now negotiated credit terms with the supplier of the asset and will be paying in equal instalments in March, April and May.

Whatever the change to estimates or assumptions that you are told about the technique is the same:

- Alter the cash receipts/payments affected
- Re-total the net cash movement
- Change the closing balance of cash in the cash budget
- Change the opening balance for the next period to reflect the altered closing cash balance in the previous period
- Carrying out this process for all subsequent periods of the cash budget.

HOW IT WORKS

We will now return again to the cash budget for the fuel division of SC Fuel and Glass (although in this example we will ignore overdraft interest for simplicity).

The cash budget to date appears as follows:

Cash budget – October to December

	October £	November £	December £
Cash receipts:			
Cash sales	136,000	140,000	150,000
Cash from credit sales	467,200	491,200	532,800
Sale of non-current (fixed) asset		9,000	9,000
Total cash receipts	603,200	640,200	691,800
Cash payments:			
Payments for credit purchases	366,960	401,700	423,450
Wages and salaries	113,000	113,000	113,000
General overheads	68,000	73,250	75,000
Capital expenditure			120,000
VAT	45,000		
Total cash payments	592,960	587,950	731,450
Net cash flow for the month	10,240	52,250	(39,650)
Opening cash balance	(29,500)	(19,260)	32,990
Closing cash balance	(19,260)	32,990	(6,660)

It has now been determined that the sale of the non-current (fixed) asset will take place in October for a cash price of £15,000. We will produce the revised budget to show the effect of this change in assumption and price.

Cash budget – October to December

	October	November	December
	£	£	£
Cash receipts:			
Cash sales	136,000	140,000	150,000
Cash from credit sales	467,200	491,200	532,800
Sale of non-current (fixed) asset	15,000		
Total cash receipts	618,200	631,200	682,800
Cash payments:			
Payments for credit purchases	366,960	401,700	423,450
Wages and salaries	113,000	113,000	113,000
General overheads	68,000	73,250	75,000
Capital expenditure			120,000
VAT	45,000		
Total cash payments	592,960	587,950	731,450
Net cash flow for the month	25,240	43,250	(48,650)
Opening cash balance	(29,500)	(4,260)	38,990
Closing cash balance	(4,260)	38,990	(9,660)

MANUFACTURING ORGANISATIONS

The cash budgets that have been prepared so far in this chapter have been based upon a retail-type organisation whereby goods are purchased for cash or on credit and then sold to customers either for cash or on credit. However, we also need to consider how to prepare a cash budget for a manufacturing organisation. In a manufacturing organisation, materials (for example, glass) are purchased in order to produce sales units (such as windows).

Cash payments

In a manufacturing organisation the major difference is in the calculations that are required in order to determine the cash payments for each period, in particular for purchases and for wages.

Purchases

The amount of purchases in each month will depend upon the amount of production in the factory each month. This will be determined by the production budget.

HOW IT WORKS

We will now consider the glass division of SC Fuel and Glass. The cash flow forecast for this division is to be prepared for the three months of October, November and December. We will start with the purchases of materials.

The glass division makes sealed double-glazed units in its factory and the material required costs £16 per unit.

The forecast sales demand of double-glazed units, are anticipated to be:

	Units
September	12,300
October	13,200
November	14,300
December	14,500

Purchases are calculated as 60% of the next month's forecast sales and are paid two months after the date of purchase. For example, purchases in September are based on the estimated sales for October and paid for in November.

Purchases

	August	September	October	November	December
Sales Demand (units)		12,300	13,200	14,300	14,500
Purchases (×60% ×£16)		118,080	126,720	137,280	139,200
Date purchase made	118,080	126,720	137,280	139,200	
Date purchase paid for			118,080	126,720	137,280

Now we can complete the first line of cash payments in the cash budget for the glass division.

Cash budget – October to December

	October	November	December
Cash Payments			
Payments to Suppliers	118,080	126,720	137,280

Changes in inventory

The example above was fairly straightforward because the purchases were just based on sales demand. Assessment questions on purchases will probably be based on sales demand.

There is a further complication, however, that you might come across and that is opening and closing inventory. A business may not sell as many units as it had hoped and may therefore be left with unsold inventory at the month end. This means that it won't need to make as many purchases in the next month because it has this head start. Sometimes a business may want to produce more units than it needs, in order to have some left in stock, just in case. Inventory left at the month end is called closing inventory. The closing inventory at the end of one month becomes the opening inventory of the next month.

Purchases (in units) are calculated as follows

	Quantity
Production required to meet sales demand	X
Less: opening inventory (stock)	(X)
Add: closing inventory (stock)	X
Purchases quantity	X

HOW IT WORKS

Table Co expects the following sales demand.

January (units)	February (units)	March (units)
800	850	900

Each unit requires 2kg of wood at a cost of £8 per kg.

Closing inventory is expected to be as follows.

December kg	January kg	February kg	March kg
350	300	400	450

The purchases quantity

	January	February	March
	kg	kg	kg
Production required to meet sales demand (demand × 2kg)	1,600	1,700	1,800
Less: opening inventory (stock)	(350)	(300)	(400)
Add: closing inventory (stock)	300	400	450
Purchases quantity	1,550	1,800	1,850

The amount in monetary terms is found by multiplying the quantity by the price per kg (£8).

	January	February	March
	£	£	£
Purchases (1,550 × £8, 1,800 × £8, 1,850 × £8)	12,400	14,400	14,800

Wages

In a manufacturing organisation the wages paid to the production workers will often be dependent upon the hours that they work and dependent upon each period's production quantity as calculated in the production budget.

HOW IT WORKS

Returning to SC Fuel and Glass and the glass division cash budget: the production director tells you that each glazed unit requires 1.5 labour hours and the payroll department informs you that the workforce is paid at a rate of £8 per hour. Gross wages are paid in the same month as they are incurred.

Using the production budget the wages cash payment each month can be calculated.

Production budget – units

	October	November	December
	Units	Units	Units
Production quantity	13,200	14,300	14,500

Gross wages payments

	October	November	December
	£	£	£
October (13,200 × 1.5 × £8)	158,400		
November (14,300 × 1.5 × £8)		171,600	
December (14,500 × 1.5 × £8)			174,000

These figures can then also be entered into the cash budget.

Cash budget – October to December

	October	November	December
	£	£	£
Cash payments:			
Payments to suppliers	118,080	126,720	137,280
Wages	158,400	171,600	174,000

Cash receipts from sales

In Chapter 3 of this Text we calculated the cash receipts from sales for the glass division of SC Fuels and Glass when we were considering the effects of bad debts. The cash receipts to appear in the cash budget were calculated as follows:

	October	November	December
	£	£	£
Cash receipts:			
Cash from credit sales	818,400	940,800	1,024,800

Cash budget – October to December

	October	November	December
	£	£	£
Cash receipts:			
Cash from credit sales	818,400	940,800	1,024,800
Cash payments:			
Payments to suppliers	118,080	126,720	137,280
Wages	158,400	171,600	174,000

Other receipts and payments

Finally to complete the cash budget the other cash receipts and payments for the period will be included.

HOW IT WORKS

The remaining figures need to be dealt with in the cash budget for the glass division.

- Production expenses are estimated as 15% of the materials and wages payments and are paid in the month in which they are incurred. This figure includes £18,000 of depreciation charge each month

- Selling costs are estimated as 10% of the sales revenue for the period and 75% are payable in the month in which they are incurred and the remainder in the following month (the sales in units were September: 12,000 units, October: 13,200 units, November: 14,100 units and December: 14,800 units. All sales were at £80 per unit)

- Additional machinery has been acquired under a lease and the lease payments are £15,000 each month

- In October the corporation tax payment of £290,000 must be paid

- The cash balance at 1 October is anticipated to be £45,000

- In this example we are ignoring the complication of overdraft interest charges or bank interest receivable

The cash budget can now be completed:

Cash budget – October to December

	October £	November £	December £
Cash receipts:			
Cash from credit sales	818,400	940,800	1,024,800
Cash payments:			
Payments to suppliers	118,080	126,720	137,280
Wages	158,400	171,600	174,000
Production expenses (W1)	23,472	26,748	28,692
Selling costs (W2)	103,200	111,000	117,000
Lease payments	15,000	15,000	15,000
Corporation tax	290,000	0	0
Total payments	708,152	451,068	471,972
Net cash flow for the month	110,248	489,732	552,828
Opening cash balance	45,000	155,248	644,980
Closing cash balance	155,248	644,980	1,197,808

WORKINGS

Working 1 – Production expenses

	October £	November £	December £
October			
((15% × (118,080 + 158,400)) – 18,000)	23,472		
November			
((15% × (126,720 + 171,600)) – 18,000)		26,748	
December			
((15% × (137,280 + 174,000)) – 18,000)			28,692

Working 2 – Selling costs

	October £	November £	December £
September costs			
(10% × (12,000 × £80) × 25%)	24,000		
October costs			
(10% × (13,200 × £80) × 75%)	79,200		
(10% × (13,200 × £80) × 25%)		26,400	
November costs			
(10% × (14,100 × £80) × 75%)		84,600	
(10% × (14,100 × £80) × 25%)			28,200
December costs			
(10% × (14,800 × £80) × 75%)			88,800
Total selling costs	103,200	111,000	117,000

Task 2

A company has negotiated new payment terms with its suppliers. The payment terms allow for settlement of 30% in the month following the purchase with the remaining payment two months after purchase.

The purchase figures are

	Period 1	Period 2	Period 3	Period 4	Period 5
	£	£	£	£	£
Purchases	21,000	24,000	24,550	27,350	27,775

Complete the table below to show the timing of the purchase payments.

	Period 3	Period 4	Period 5
Period 1	14700		
Period 2	7200		
Period 2		16,800	
Period 3		7365	17725
Period 3			17185
Period 4			8205
	21900	24165	25390

CHAPTER OVERVIEW

- In order to prepare a cash budget information will be required from many different sources within the organisation.

- Care must be taken with the timing of other cash flows such as overheads which may not necessarily be all paid in the month incurred – any non-cash flows such as depreciation charges must be excluded from the cash flow forecast.

- If information is given about overdraft interest then this must be calculated each month based upon the overdraft balance at the start of the month and shown as a cash outflow.

- If information is given about bank interest receivable on credit balances then this must be calculated based upon the balance at the start of the month and shown as a cash inflow.

- If there are changes in estimates or assumptions used in the cash budget then these must be put through with an altered cash budget in subsequent periods.

- In a manufacturing organisation the amount of payments for purchases will be dependent upon the production budget and the purchases pattern and supplier payment pattern.

- In a manufacturing organisation the wages payment for the period may also be dependent upon the production quantity each period.

Keywords

Purchases budget – a budget showing the purchases required in units to meet the production budget and any planned changes to closing inventories (stock) of raw materials.

TEST YOUR LEARNING

Test 1

A business is about to prepare a cash budget for the quarter ending 31 December. The estimated sales figures are as follows:

	£
September (estimate)	360,000
October (estimate)	400,000
November (estimate)	450,000
December (estimate)	460,000

All sales are on credit and the payment pattern is as follows:

20% pay in the month of sale after taking a 5% settlement discount

80% pay in the month following the sale

(a) **Complete the table below in order to calculate the receipts from credit sales for the quarter ending 31 December.**

	October	November	December
	£	£	£
	288.000		
	76.000		
		320,000	
		85.500	
			360,000
			87.400
	364.000	405 500	447.400

The purchases of the business are all on credit and it is estimated that the following purchases will be made:

	£
August	200,000
September	220,000
October	240,000
November	270,000
December	280,000

30% of purchases are paid for in the month after the purchase has been made and the remainder are paid for two months after the month of purchase.

(b) **Complete the table below to calculate the payments for purchases on credit for the three months ending 31 December.**

	October	November	December
	£	£	£
	140,000		
	66.000		
		154.000	
		72000	
			168.000
			81.000
	206.000	226.000	249.000

General overheads are anticipated to be £30,000 for each of September and October increasing to £36,000 thereafter. 80% of the general overheads are paid for in the month in which they are incurred and the remainder in the following month. Included in the general overheads figure is a depreciation charge of £5,000 each month.

(c) **Complete the table below to calculate the cash payments for general overheads for each month for the three months ending 31 December.**

	October	November	December
	£	£	£
	5000		
	20000		
		5000	
		24800	
			6200
			24800
	25000	29800	31000

Additional information

- Gross wages are expected to be £42,000 each month and are paid in the month in which they are incurred.

- Selling expenses are anticipated to be 5% of the monthly sales value and are paid for in the month following the sale.

- The business has planned to purchase new equipment for £40,000 in November and in the same month to dispose of old equipment with estimated sales proceeds of £4,000.

- If the business has an overdraft balance at the start of the month then there is an interest charge that month of 1% of the overdraft balance. At 1 October it is anticipated that the business will have an overdraft of £50,000.

(d) **Referring to your answers in parts (a), (b) and (c) and the additional information above prepare a monthly cash budget for the three months ending 31 December. Cash inflows should be entered as positive figures and cash outflows as negative figures.**

Cash budget for the quarter ending 31 December

	October	November	December
	£	£	£
Cash receipts			
Sales proceeds from equipment	0	4000	0
Receipts from sales	364000	405500	447400
Total receipts	364000	409500	447400
Cash payments			
Payments for purchases	206000	226000	249000
Wages	42000	42000	42000
General overheads	25000	29800	31000
Selling expenses	18000	20,000	22500
New equipment	0	40000	0
Overdraft interest	500	0	0
Total payments	291500	357800	344500
Net cash flow	72500	51700	102900
Opening balance	(50,000)	22500	74200
Closing balance	22500	74200	177100

Test 2

A manufacturing business is to prepare its cash budget for the three months commencing 1 October. The business manufactures a product called the gleep which requires two hours of labour per completed gleep. The labour force is paid at a rate of £7.50 per hour. Each gleep sells for £60.

The forecast sales in gleeps are as follows:

Forecast sales – units of gleeps

August	September	October	November	December
7,000	7,200	6,800	7,400	7,500

Sales are on credit with 60% of customers paying in the month after sale and the remainder two months after the sale.

The production for gleeps is as follows (units):

September	October	November	December
7,200	6,700	7,300	7,400

(a) **Complete the table below to calculate the cash receipts from sales for the three months ending December.**

	October	November	December
	£	£	£
	168,000		
	259,200		
		172,800	
		244,800	
			163,200
			266,400
Total receipts from sales	427,200	417,600	429,600

The raw materials required for production are purchased in the month prior to production and 40% are paid for in the following month and the remainder two months after purchase. Purchase figures are as follows:

	£
September	172,800
October	163,200
November	178,800
December	175,200

(b) **Complete the table below to calculate the amount paid for purchases in each of the three months from October to December.**

	October	November	December
	£	£	£
	69120		
		103680	
		65.280	
			97920
			71520
Total payments for purchases	69120	168960	169440

Additional information

- The production staff gross wages are paid in the month in which they are incurred.

- Production overheads are anticipated to be 40% of the materials purchased each month and are paid for in the month in which they are incurred.

- General overheads are anticipated to be £64,000 in each of October and November increasing to £70,000 in December and are paid in the month in which they are incurred. The figure for general overheads includes £12,000 of depreciation each month.

- The cash balance at 1 October is expected to be £20,000 in credit.

(c) **Referring to your answers to parts (a) and (b) and the additional information above prepare a monthly cash budget for the three months ending December. Cash inflows should be entered as positive figures and cash outflows as negative figures.**

	October	November	December
	£	£	£
Cash receipts			
Sales	427200	419600	429600
Cash payments			
Purchases	=69120	-168960	-169440
Wages	-100500	-109500	-111000
Production overheads	-65280	-71520	-70080
General overheads	-52000	-52000	-58000
Total payments	-286900	-401980	-408520
Net cash flow	140300	15620	21080
Opening balance	20,000	160.300	175920
Closing balance	160.300	175920	197000

chapter 6:
MANAGING CASH SHORTAGES

chapter coverage 📖

As we have seen in the last chapter of this Text a cash budget is a useful method of determining whether it is likely that the business will have enough cash to keep going. If a cash deficit is forecast in the cash budget then management will be able to find suitable financing options to cover this deficit. In this chapter we look at some of the financing options available to businesses to cover cash shortages but we start with a general consideration of how the banking system and money markets work which is essential background information.

The topics covered are:

✎ The banking system

✎ Relationship of the bank and the customer

✎ Money markets

✎ Dealing with a cash deficit

✎ Raising additional finance

✎ Overdraft finance

✎ Short-term bank loan

THE BANKING SYSTEM

If a business is to raise additional funds or invest surplus funds then this will be done either through a bank or within the money markets. Therefore we will begin this chapter with a look at the banking system in the UK and the money markets.

Banks

There are two main types of banks in the UK, primary and secondary banks.

PRIMARY BANKS are those which operate the money transmission service in the economy. This means that they are the banks which operate cheque accounts and deal with cheque clearing. They are sometimes also known as the commercial, retail or clearing banks.

The SECONDARY BANKS are made up of a wide range of merchant banks, other British banks and foreign banks in the UK. They do not tend to take part in the cheque clearing system.

Financial intermediation

Banks take deposits from customers and then use those funds to lend money to other customers. This process is known as FINANCIAL INTERMEDIATION. The banks act effectively as middlemen providing funds for those that want loans from the deposits made by savers.

The main benefits of financial intermediation are as follows:

- Small amounts deposited by savers can be combined to provide larger loan packages to businesses

- Short-term savings can be transferred into long-term borrowings

- Search costs are reduced as companies seeking loan finance can approach a bank directly rather than finding individuals to lend to them

- Risk is reduced as an individual's savings are not tied up with one individual borrower directly

Assets of banks

When individuals or companies pay money into their accounts with a bank then the bank, of course, has that money as an asset. However, these assets of a retail bank come in a variety of different forms:

- Notes and coin – branches require notes and coins to meet demands for withdrawals by customers

- Balances with the Bank of England. There are two types of such balances – cash ratio deposits and operational deposits. The cash ratio deposit is a requirement of the Bank of England that a certain percentage of a bank's deposits must be held with the Bank of England. Operational deposits are the funds required to meet each bank's obligations under the clearing system for cheque payments

- Bills. The banks will tend to hold very low risk bills. These include the following:

    - Treasury bills – three-month loans issued by the Bank of England on behalf of the government (see later in the chapter)

    - Local authority bills which are similar to Treasury bills but are issued by local government (see later in the chapter)

    - Commercial bills of exchange which are a promise by one firm to pay another a stated amount on a certain day (see later in the chapter)

- Loans to customers and overdrafts of customers

- Loans to the money markets or other banks

- Securities

Liabilities of banks

The liabilities of the banks are the amounts that customers have paid into the bank in the form of their account balances.

Task 1

What are the main advantages of financial intermediation?

-

-

-

-

Relationship of the bank and the customer

When money is paid into a bank by an individual or business and an account is opened then that individual or business becomes a customer of the bank.

The legal relationship between the bank and its customer is quite complex and there are potentially four main contractual relationships between the bank and the customer:

- The (receivable/payable) relationship
- The bailor/bailee relationship
- The principal/agent relationship
- The mortgagor/mortgagee relationship

Receivable/ payable (debtor/creditor) relationship

When the customer deposits money the bank becomes the receivable (debtor) and the customer a payable (creditor) of the bank. If the customer's account is overdrawn however, the bank becomes the payable (creditor) and the customer the receivable (debtor).

This relationship is essentially a contract between the bank and the customer and there are a number of essential areas in this contract:

- The bank borrows the customer's deposits and undertakes to repay them

- The bank must receive cheques for the customer's account

- The bank will only cease to do business with the customer with reasonable notice

- The bank is not liable to pay until the customer demands payment

- The customer exercises reasonable care when writing cheques

Bailor/bailee relationship

This element of the relationship between customer and bank concerns the bank accepting the customer's property for storage in its safe deposit. The bank will undertake to take reasonable care to safeguard the property against loss or damage and also to re-deliver it only to the customer or someone authorised by the customer.

Principal/agent relationship

An agent is someone who acts on behalf of another party, the principal. Within banking the principal/agent relationship exists where, for example, the customer pays a crossed cheque into the bank. The bank acts as an agent when, as receiving bank, it presents the cheque for payment to the paying bank, and then pays the proceeds into the customer's account.

Mortgagor/mortgagee relationship

If the bank asks the customer to secure a loan with a charge over its assets then the relationship between the two is that of mortgagor and mortgagee. If the customer does not repay the loan then the bank has the right to sell the assets and use the proceeds to pay off the loan.

Fiduciary relationship

The bank and the customer also have a fiduciary relationship which means that the bank is expected to act with the utmost good faith in its relationship with the customer.

The duties of the bank

The bank has a number of duties to its customers which include the following:

- It must honour a customer's cheque provided it is correctly made out, there is no legal reason for not honouring it and the customer has enough funds or overdraft limit to cover the amount of the cheque

- The bank must credit cash/cheques that are paid in to the customer's account

- If the customer makes a written request for repayment of funds in their account, for example by writing a cheque, the bank must repay the amount on demand

- The bank must comply with the customer's instructions given by direct debit mandate or standing order

- The bank must provide a statement showing the transactions on the account within a reasonable period and provide details of the balance on the customer's account

- The bank must respect the confidentiality of the customer's affairs unless the bank is required by law, public duty or its own interest to disclose details or where the customer gives their consent for such disclosure

- The bank must tell the customer if there has been an attempt to forge the customer's signature on a cheque

- The bank should use care and skill in its actions

- The bank must provide reasonable notice if it is to close a customer's account.

Customer's duties

The customer also has duties in respect of their dealings with their bank. The two main duties are:

- To draw up cheques carefully so that fraud is not facilitated
- To tell the bank of any known forgeries.

The rights of the bank

The services that the bank provides are, of course, performed as part of its business and as such the bank has certain rights:

- To charge reasonable bank charges and commissions over and above interest

- To use the customer's money in any way provided that it is legal and morally acceptable

- To be repaid overdrawn balances on demand (although the bank will rarely enforce this)

- To be indemnified against possible losses when acting on a customer's behalf.

Task 2

Which of the following are the customer's duties when dealing with the bank?

A   To ensure that they have funds in the bank

B   Not to exceed an overdraft limit

C   To tell the bank of any known forgeries

D   Only to write cheques when there are funds in the account

---

MONEY MARKETS

The MONEY MARKETS cover a vast array of markets buying and selling different forms of money or marketable securities. MARKETABLE SECURITIES are short-term highly liquid investments that are readily convertible into cash. The money markets provide the financial institutions with a means of borrowing and investing to deal with short-term fluctuations in their own assets and liabilities.

The main traders in the money markets are banks, the government through the Bank of England, local authorities, brokers and other intermediaries in the market.

Money market financial instruments

There are a variety of different financial instruments that are traded in the money markets. The main types are:

- Bills – short-term financial assets that can be converted into cash by selling them in the discount market

- Deposits – money in the bank accounts of banks and other financial intermediaries

- Commercial paper – IOUs issued by large companies which can be either held to maturity or sold to third parties before maturity

- Certificates of deposit (CDs) – a certificate for deposit of £50,000 or more for a fixed term which can be sold earlier than maturity in the CD market (dealt with later in this Text).

The primary market

A PRIMARY MARKET is where new financial instruments are issued for cash, whereas a SECONDARY MARKET is where existing financial instruments are traded between participants in the market. The Bank of England uses the primary market to smooth out fluctuations in its weekly cash balances by selling Treasury bills to banks and securities firms if it needs to raise money, or by buying back Treasury bills if it has surplus money.

The local authority market

In this market local government authorities borrow short-term funds by issuing local authority bills with a maturity of about one year or shorter.

The inter-bank market

This is a market for very short-term borrowing, often overnight, between the banks. It is used to smooth fluctuations in the banks' receipts and payments. The interest rate charged in this market is the LONDON INTER-BANK OFFERED RATE (LIBOR). The individual banks then use this rate in order to set their own base rate which determines the interest rate that they will offer to their own customers.

Task 3

Use the picklist to complete the following sentence.

A secondary money market is one where [new financial instruments are issued/existing financial instruments are traded].

DEALING WITH A CASH DEFICIT

As we have seen, preparation of the cash budget or cash flow forecast may highlight a point in the future where the business will be short of funds, ie a CASH DEFICIT. In some cases the senior management of the business may also be able to identify a time when additional finance will be required even before a cash budget is prepared, for example if a Board decision is made to purchase a new property or acquire another business.

For the purposes of this syllabus it is important that you appreciate:

- The various forms of finance that are available to deal with a cash deficit; and
- How to determine the most appropriate type of finance for the particular purpose.

First, therefore, you have to know why the additional finance is required.

Possible reasons for additional finance

There are many reasons why a business may have a cash deficit or need to raise additional finance. The most common being to:

- Fund day-to-day working capital
    - Increase inventory (stock) or sales levels (and therefore receivables (debtors))
    - Reduce payables (creditors)
- Purchase non-current (fixed) assets
- Acquire another business

The need to raise the finance may be highlighted by a deficit in the cash budget, by management decisions regarding investment in non-current (fixed) assets or by the business strategy of growth by acquisition.

Funding working capital

One of the most common reasons for additional finance which is normally highlighted by a deficit in the cash budget is in order to fund the day-to-day working capital of the business. All businesses have a working capital/cash cycle (see Chapter 1 of this Text) which is effectively the period between the payment of money for goods to suppliers and the receipt of money for sales from customers.

If suppliers are being paid more quickly than money is being received from customers then it is likely that at some point the business will require funds to cover the period until the money from customers is received.

Increasing working capital

After a period of operating, a business may find that it needs an increase in its working capital. This could be due to a number of reasons:

- Increase in sales turnover
- Increase in receivables (debtors)
- Increase in inventory (stock)
- Reduction of payables (creditors)

Increase in sales turnover

If sales turnover increases then this will often require increases in both inventory (stock) and receivables (debtors). The business may be able to gain additional credit from its trade payables (creditors) but in the absence of that may have to raise funds to finance this increase.

Increase in receivables (debtors)

The additional finance required might be due to an increase in receivables (debtors). This could have been due to inefficiencies in the credit control of the business or it may have been necessary to increase the credit period and credit amount offered to customers, in order to keep their custom in a competitive market or to increase market share and sales turnover.

Increase in inventory (stock)

Sometimes, additional finance might be required due to an increase in inventory (stock) levels which is not due to a general increase in turnover. These types of inventory (stock) increases will normally only be temporary and could be due to any of the following:

- Taking advantage of an attractive price by placing a bulk order

- Building up inventory (stock) in advance of a peak period in a seasonal business

- Receipt of a large order from a customer for which supplies must be purchased.

Reduction of payables (creditors)

In some cases, a business may find that it needs to reduce its trade payables (creditors) either to take advantage of settlement discounts or because trade payables (creditors) may be pressing the business for quicker payment for their own reasons. This reduction in trade credit will need to be funded by some other source of finance as the taking of credit from suppliers is effectively a source of finance for a business.

In other cases, additional finance may be required in the short term to fund payments such as the quarterly VAT or the annual corporation tax due if cash has not been put aside for such purposes.

Purchase of non-current (fixed) assets

We have seen in the last few paragraphs that there are many reasons why a business may need additional finance in order to fund its working capital and the need for this finance will normally have been highlighted by a budgeted deficit in the cash budget.

However, most businesses will need to invest in additional or replacement non-current (fixed) assets on a fairly regular basis. In many cases a business will not be able to purchase the non-current (fixed) assets required to maintain or expand operations out of cash and will therefore need to raise finance in order to fund the purchase.

Acquisition of another business

Many businesses have a policy of growth by acquisition of other firms. Other businesses may not generally have such a policy but, on occasion, a potential acquisition may occur. Such a major amount of expenditure will almost always require funding by some form of external finance.

RAISING ADDITIONAL FINANCE

Once the reasons for the cash deficit or the need for additional finance has been identified the next stage is to determine the type of funding required by assessing the various forms of finance that are available and determining which is most appropriate.

The form of finance required

There are many forms of external finance that are available to a business however what is important is that the most appropriate form of finance is sought for the purpose for which the finance is required. We must therefore consider the objective of the finance and also any internal regulations within the business regarding financing. For example, a business may have a policy of ensuring that there is always a cash balance or undrawn overdraft facility of £50,000 available as a back-up.

The forms of finance available will normally be classified according to their time-scale or maturity and generally can be categorised according to their term:

- Short term – anything up to three years
- Medium term – three to ten years
- Long term – over ten years

We will consider all three of these types of finance but, as a general rule, the time-scale of the finance should match the time-scale of the reason for the finance. So, if the funding is required for working capital reasons then the finance should be short term, whereas if it is required for longer-term investment in non-current (fixed) assets or another business then the appropriate time-scale may be medium or long term.

Short-term financing

The two main sources of short-term financing are an OVERDRAFT or a short-term LOAN.

OVERDRAFT FINANCE

Most of us are familiar with the concept of an overdraft, which is a form of short-term borrowing from the bank available to both business and personal customers. If a bank is approached for an overdraft then it will normally agree an OVERDRAFT FACILITY. This is the amount by which the business's account is allowed to be overdrawn. It is then up to the customer to determine how much of this overdraft facility is to be used by having an actual overdraft.

HOW IT WORKS

The fuel division of SC Fuel and Glass has an overdraft facility with its bank of £50,000. However for the three months of October, November and December the anticipated cash balances at the end of each month are:

October	£19,260 overdrawn
November	£32,990 in credit
December	£6,660 overdrawn

Therefore the finance is available from the bank up to a total of £50,000 but the business does not anticipate having to borrow all of this money in the near future.

Features of overdraft finance

There are various features of overdraft finance with which you should be familiar.

- Overdraft facility and actual overdraft – as we have seen there is a distinction between the overdraft facility offered by the bank and the actual overdraft that the business makes use of

- Interest – the interest charged on an overdraft is usually at quite a high margin over and above the bank's base rate. However interest is only charged on the amount of the actual overdraft, calculated on a daily basis, rather than on the total overdraft facility

- Commitment fee – in some cases an initial fee will be charged for the granting of the overdraft facility

- Repayment – technically an overdraft is repayable on demand to the bank. However, in practice, it would be rare for a bank to enforce this.

SHORT-TERM BANK LOAN

A short-term loan with a bank can usually be arranged rather than an overdraft. This is a loan for a fixed amount, for an agreed period of time on pre-arranged terms. Such a loan is normally taken out with formal documentation and includes details of:

- The term of the loan

- The interest rate

- The way in which the interest is charged (it may be a fixed rate, or vary in line with the base rate)

- The repayment date/dates

- Any security required for the loan

- Any covenants attached to the loan

We will now briefly consider each of these areas.

Term of the loan

The term of the loan will normally be the subject of negotiations between the customer and the bank. If the purpose of the loan is for the support of working capital or the day-to-day operations of the business then the bank will normally expect to be provided with detailed profit and cash flow projections which will indicate the most appropriate term and time-scale for repayment of the loan.

If the loan is required for the purchase of non-current (fixed) assets then the term of the loan should not normally exceed the useful life of the related non-current (fixed) assets as the loan will effectively be serviced and repaid out of the profits made by these assets.

Interest

The rate of interest on the loan will normally be set in relation to the bank's base rate which in turn is related to LIBOR. The interest may be VARIABLE RATE INTEREST or FIXED RATE INTEREST. Variable rate interest is where the interest rate charged on the loan amount changes every time the bank's own base rate changes. Fixed rate interest is a set amount that is to be charged for the entire term of the loan.

In general terms, if interest rates are expected to rise in the near future a fixed rate of interest would be preferable to a business, but if interest rates are anticipated to fall then a variable rate could be a cheaper option. A CAPPED RATE is one which is variable but is only allowed to rise to a certain amount before it becomes fixed.

Repayment terms

Loans can normally be repaid in three different ways:

- BULLET REPAYMENTS – the full amount of the loan remains outstanding for the entire term of the loan and the full amount is then repaid at the end of this period. Interest is charged on the full loan amount throughout the loan term.

- BALLOON REPAYMENTS – under this method some of the loan principal is repaid during the term of the loan but the majority is repaid at the end of the loan period. Interest will be charged on the loan amount outstanding at any point in time.

- AMORTISING REPAYMENTS – in this case the loan principal is gradually repaid over the term of the loan until there is no principal outstanding at the end of the loan period. Each regular repayment will therefore consist of some loan principal and interest on the amount still outstanding.

Security

In many cases the bank will require the business to provide security for the loan. This may take the form of a FIXED CHARGE or a FLOATING CHARGE over the business's assets.

A fixed charge is where the security is a specific asset or group of assets which the business cannot sell during the term of the loan without the bank's permission. If the business defaults on the loan then the bank can sell the asset in order to repay the outstanding amount.

A floating charge is a charge on a certain group of assets of the business, such as receivables (debtors) or inventory (stock), which will be constantly changing. If the business defaults on the loan then the bank has the right to be repaid from the proceeds of the pledged assets. Usually only a company can give a floating charge, not a sole trader or most forms of partnership.

From the bank's point of view the security that it has for a loan should have an identifiable value which is either stable or increasing, and which can be sold relatively easily and quickly to convert it into cash.

Often a sole trader or partners in a partnership will be required to give personal guarantees for the money loaned. This means that, should the business fail to make payments when due, the individual guarantor will be required to pay from personal assets.

Covenants

In the terms of some loans the bank will insist on certain obligations or restrictions on the business which are known as COVENANTS. Examples of specific loan covenants may include:

- Agreement by the business to take out no further loans until the current one has been repaid

- Agreement by the business to provide regular management accounts and cash flow forecasts to the bank during the term of the loan

- Agreement by the business that its total loans must not exceed a set percentage of its capital employed during the term of the loan

Facility letter

All of these matters and all of the legal rights and duties of either a loan or an overdraft agreement are set out in a FACILITY LETTER. This is a legal document which is signed by the bank and by the customer.

Task 4

Which of the following are features of overdraft finance?

A   Bullet repayments

B   Repayment on a set date

C   Floating charge over assets

D   Repayable on demand

Overdraft or bank loan?

As we have seen, for relatively short-term borrowing, businesses will tend to have a choice between overdraft finance or a short-term loan. Which is most appropriate?

In general terms, the financing method should be matched to the life of the asset for which the financing is required. In most cases, therefore, an overdraft is most suitable for increased working capital requirements and a loan is more suitable for the purchase of non-current (fixed) assets or another business.

You need to appreciate the advantages and disadvantages of each of these two main sources of short-term finance.

Advantages of a bank overdraft

A bank overdraft as a source of short-term funding has a number of advantages:

- Flexibility – the full overdraft facility does not need to be used and therefore the precise amount of funding required does not need to be estimated provided that the facility granted is greater than the anticipated amount of overdraft requirement. If necessary an application can be made to the bank to increase an overdraft facility at some point in the future.

- Cost – although the interest rate on an overdraft may be higher than the interest rate negotiated for a loan, the overdraft interest paid is calculated daily on the amount of the actual overdraft rather than on a fixed amount for a loan.

- Short-term – technically an overdraft is repayable on demand and therefore should normally only be used to fund short-term working capital requirements. The benefit of this is that when the short-term funding requirement is over the overdraft facility is simply not required. There is no necessity to negotiate paying-off a loan early or incurring a penalty for early repayment.

Disadvantages of a bank overdraft

However, there are also some drawbacks to the use of overdraft finance:

- Repayable on demand – technically the overdraft is repayable on demand and if the bank considers that the business performance is not in line with its cash flow forecasts or business plans then the bank can cancel the overdraft facility and require any outstanding amount to be repaid possibly causing major cash flow problems for the business.

- Increasing the facility – once an overdraft facility has been agreed with the bank it may be difficult to persuade the bank to increase that facility if additional finance is required.

- Short-term – as the overdraft is repayable on demand it is only really suitable for the financing of short-term assets such as investment in additional working capital rather than longer-term assets such as non-current (fixed) assets or acquisition of another business.

- Cost – if the full extent of the facility is consistently used, the interest payment will be higher than on a loan of the same amount.

Advantage of loan finance

The main advantage of short-term loan finance is that it can be tailored to meet the precise requirements of the business. It can be taken out for a period which matches the assets which it is financing and the repayment terms can be negotiated to correspond with the cash flows from the asset or the other business cash flows.

Disadvantages of loan finance

The potential disadvantages of short-term loan finance include:

- Cost – if the interest on a loan is fixed rate then this can sometimes be more expensive than interest on an overdraft. Also on a loan the interest charge is based upon the full amount of the loan outstanding whereas with an overdraft interest is only charged on the amount of the overdraft facility actually being used at the current time.

- Security – the bank will normally require some form of security for the loan, either a fixed or a floating charge (from a company) or a personal guarantee.

- Covenants – as we have seen the bank may impose certain restrictions or covenants which will limit the freedom of action of the management of the business.

Medium-term bank loans

On the whole medium-term debt finance should be used to fund the purchase of assets with a three to ten year life such as plant and machinery. However, it can also be useful to fund a medium-term deficit in working capital.

The terms of such a loan will be similar to those for a short-term loan covering areas such as interest, repayment, security and covenants.

Medium-term loans and working capital

As we have seen, in most cases, a bank loan is most appropriate for the purchase of major assets which will hopefully provide income over the loan period out of which the loan interest and repayments can be made. However in some situations it may be necessary to raise a medium-term loan to finance a working capital deficit.

Suppose that a business has consistently had an overdraft of between £50,000 and £70,000 for the last 18 months. This would appear to be part of the permanent funding capital of the business and would be known as the HARDCORE OVERDRAFT. Overdraft interest tends to be at a higher rate than loan interest as an overdraft is harder to monitor from the bank's perspective and tends to be more volatile. Therefore this company might convert the hardcore overdraft into say a £70,000 five year loan which will be paid off over the period but which should reduce the amount of overdraft finance required.

Task 5

Which are the main types of conditions that would appear in a loan agreement with a bank?

- (i) The term of the loan
- (ii) The interest rate
- (iii) The way in which interest is charged
- (iv) The repayment schedule
- (v) Any security required
- (vi) Any covenants stipulated

A (i), (iii), (v) and (vi)
B (ii), (iii), (iv) and (v)
C (i), (ii), (iv) and (vi)
D All of them

CHAPTER OVERVIEW

- One of the primary purposes of the banking system is that of financial intermediation.

- The assets of the banks take a variety of forms including cash, deposits held with the Bank of England, bills, loans and overdrafts – the liabilities of the bank are its customers' account balances.

- There are four potential contractual relationships between a bank and its customer with the most important being the receivable/ payable (debtor/ creditor) relationship.

- Not only do banks have a number of duties to their customers but the customers also have a duty to take care to ensure that fraud is not facilitated.

- The money markets are a vast array of markets buying and selling different forms of cash and marketable securities.

- Once a forecast cash deficit is identified the reason for the deficit must first be determined in order to identify the most appropriate source of finance.

- A cash deficit is often caused by working capital problems or by the need to fund an increasing cash cycle – in other cases the cash deficit may be due to the need to purchase non-current (fixed) assets or even acquire another business.

- Over the short term the two main sources of additional finance are either overdraft finance or a loan.

- An overdraft facility may be granted by the bank and the business can then run an overdraft of any amount up to that facility total – interest will be charged only on the amount of the actual overdraft on a daily basis.

- If loan finance is taken out the loan agreement or facility letter will include details of the term of the loan, the interest rate, the repayment pattern, any security and any covenants.

- The choice between an overdraft or a loan will normally depend upon the reason for the deficit – in general, a deficit due to working capital shortages will be financed by an overdraft but if the deficit is for the purchase of longer-term non-current (fixed) assets a loan to match the life of the assets would be more appropriate.

KEY WORDS

Primary banks – the high street or retail banks

Secondary banks – banks other than the primary banks operating in the UK

Financial intermediation – the process of banks taking deposits from customers to lend to others

Money markets – markets buying and selling different forms of money and marketable securities

Marketable securities – short-term, highly liquid investments readily convertible into cash

Primary market – new financial instruments are issued for cash

Secondary market – existing financial instruments are traded between participants in the market.

London Inter-Bank Offered Rate (LIBOR) – the interest rate prevailing in the London inter-bank market

Cash deficit – shortage of cash

Overdraft – the amount by which a customer's bank account is in debit

Overdraft facility – the amount of potential overdraft that a bank allows a customer

Loan – an amount of money advanced by a bank to its customer

Variable rate interest – interest on a loan which changes every time the bank changes its base rate

Fixed rate interest – an agreed fixed rate of interest for the term of a loan

Capped rate interest – variable interest allowed to rise until a certain level prevails when it becomes a fixed rate

Bullet repayments – the entire loan is paid off at the end of the loan period with only interest payments made during the term of the loan

Balloon repayments – some loan principal is paid off during the term of the loan but most of it at the end of the loan period

Amortising repayments – repayments are made up of interest and principal so that there is no principal remaining at the end of the loan term

Fixed charge – security for the loan is a specific asset which cannot be sold without the bank's permission

Floating charge – charge on a group of assets that are constantly changing such as receivables (debtors) or inventory (stock)

Covenants – obligations or restrictions placed on the business by the loan provider

Facility letters – a formal document signed by both the bank and the customer setting out the legal rights and duties relating to loan or overdraft finance

Hardcore overdraft – an overdraft which has effectively become a permanent part of the capital of the business

TEST YOUR LEARNING

Test 1

Which of the following is not a potential contractual relationships between a bank and its customer.

A Trustee/beneficiary
B Principal/agent
C Mortgagor/mortgagee
D Bailor/bailee

Test 2

Which of the following are not part of the main duties of a bank in relation to its customers?

A Honour the customer's cheque provided it is correctly made out
B Grant an overdraft when requested
C Respect the confidentiality of the customer's affairs
D Provide a statement showing the transactions on the customer's account within a reasonable period

Test 3

Using the picklist complete the following sentence.

LIBOR stands for [lowest intra-bank operating rate/London inter-bank offered rate/London inter-bank operating rate].

Test 4

Compare overdraft finance with that of a loan.

Which of the following would be advantages of overdraft finance?

Tick the appropriate boxes.

Floating charge required

Interest charged only on amount of facility used

Repayable on demand

Test 5

A Ltd is considering the purchase of shares in B Ltd which will require external finance and will be held for a number of years.

What would be the most appropriate source of finance for this purchase?

A   Overdraft finance

(B)   Loan finance

Test 6

What are the three main repayment patterns of repaying a loan?

- BULLET
- BALLOON
- AMORTISING

Test 7

Using the picklists complete the following sentence.

A fixed charge is security against the [non-current (fixed) assets/current assets] of a business.

chapter 7:
MANAGING SURPLUS FUNDS

---

chapter coverage 📖

In a similar way to selecting suitable finance for dealing with cash shortages organisations also need to utilise cash surpluses in the most appropriate manner in order to ensure that they maximise return for the minimum level of risk.

The topics covered are:

- ✎ Dealing with a cash surplus
- ✎ Types of investment
- ✎ Government monetary policy
- ✎ Dealing with cash

DEALING WITH A CASH SURPLUS

In some instances the cash budget may highlight a period in time where the business has a CASH SURPLUS, which is money held in its current bank account. In most cases, money in a current account is not earning any interest or at least a very low rate of interest. It is known as an idle asset. Such cash is effectively not working for the business and should be invested to earn profits.

The cash budget will highlight the anticipated amount of the cash surplus and the anticipated period during which there will be a cash surplus so the business can plan how to invest such funds most effectively.

There are three main factors that should be considered when determining how to invest any surplus funds:

- Risk
- Return
- Liquidity

Risk

RISK is the chance that the business will make a loss on its investment. For example, a business invests £20,000 of surplus cash by buying 10,000 shares in another company at £2 per share. It then sells the shares two months later when the cash is required for operational purposes. The share price may have increased to £2.20 per share giving proceeds of £22,000 but there is also the risk that the shares will have decreased in value to say £1.90 per share meaning that only £19,000 is realised and the business has made a loss of £1,000.

When cash is invested there are two main risks. There is the risk that the value of the investment will fall (as above) which is the CAPITAL RISK. There is also the risk that the return from the investment will be lower than expected due to changes in market rates of return.

Return

The RETURN on an investment has two potential aspects – the INCOME RETURN and the CAPITAL RETURN. Most investments will pay some form of interest or dividend which is the income return. However most investments will also tend to fluctuate in value over time and this is the capital return (or capital loss).

Liquidity

LIQUIDITY is the term used for the ease and speed with which an investment can be converted into cash. Any investments which are widely traded on a market, such as the money markets, will be very liquid but investments such as a bank deposit account which requires three months' notice to withdraw the funds would not be a liquid investment.

With investments there tends to be a relationship between each of these three elements of risk, return and liquidity.

Risk and return

As a general rule risk and return are related: the higher the risk of an investment, the higher will be its anticipated return. Most businesses which have surplus funds to invest will want those funds to earn a good profit or return but will not wish to take unnecessary risks. The safety of the value of the asset will also be of great importance.

HOW IT WORKS

The glass division of SC Fuel and Glass has £60,000 to invest for the next month until the money is needed to pay the quarterly VAT bill. It could be paid into an interest-bearing deposit account at the bank where it will earn 0.5% interest for the month. Alternatively, it could be used to buy shares in another company.

If it is paid into the deposit account then the money bears virtually no risk at all (provided that the bank is creditworthy). One month later the money will be withdrawn and will total:

£60,000 + (60,000 × 0.005) = £60,300

The business has made a profit or return of £300 and the money is available to pay the VAT bill.

If the shares were purchased then it is possible that they would have increased in value to say £66,000 in one month's time meaning that the glass division has earned a profit of £6,000. However it is also possible, due to the risk of investment in shares, that the shares might have fallen in value to £55,000. This would mean that not only has the glass division made a loss of £5,000 but the full amount of cash is not available to meet the VAT bill.

Task 1

Using the picklists complete the following sentence.

The general relationship between risk and return with investments is that the [higher/lower] the risk the [higher/lower] the return.

Return and liquidity

As we have seen if any surplus cash is invested it is important to ensure that it can be realised, ie converted back into cash, when needed.

The ease of this conversion back into cash will be reflected in the return that the investment gives. If an investment cannot be quickly or easily realised then it will normally give a higher return in compensation for this. If a business has a cash surplus and is certain that it will not need the cash for a particular period of time then it will usually be able to earn a higher return than an investment where the cash can be realised immediately if required.

For example the interest earned on a bank deposit account which requires a month's notice for any withdrawal will be higher than the interest on a deposit account where the funds can be withdrawn at any time.

Risk, return and liquidity

In conclusion, therefore, when a cash surplus is to be invested the aim will be to earn a good return but without incurring excessive risk of loss and also ensuring that the investment can be realised within the time-scale in which the cash is required.

Organisational rules and procedures

In most companies there will be certain regulations and procedures to ensure that the liquidity of the business is safeguarded. Typical of such rules and procedures may be the following:

- A certain amount of cash to be available immediately at any point in time
- Investments in certain types of instrument limited to a particular financial amount
- Surplus funds might only be allowed to be invested in certain specified types of investment
- All investments must be convertible into cash within a certain number of days

Any such procedures, regulations and limits must be followed at all times. In some cases there may also be statutory regulations affecting the investments of a company but if that is the case these will be given to you in a computer based assessment.

In larger organisations there is likely to be a separate treasury function which is responsible for dealing with liquidity management and the investment of funds. It will be this function of the organisation which has the responsibility for ensuring the minimum requirements for liquidity in the organisation are met and that any investments are within the organisation's rules and regulations and offer the best return/risk/liquidity available.

TYPES OF INVESTMENT

In the previous section we looked at the general considerations that must be taken into account when investing any surplus cash. In this section we consider the possible types of investment which may be suitable for any cash surplus a business may have.

Bank or building society deposit accounts

One of the safest forms of investment for surplus cash is to pay it into a high street bank or building society deposit account. Retail banks and building societies offer a wide range of such accounts although the interest rate, particularly for small sums, is generally quite low. Online accounts tend to attract a higher interest rate.

There are higher interest deposit accounts for larger amounts, for example provided that there is always a balance of say £10,000 in the account. Access to the cash is usually immediate and therefore useful if cash requirements are not known for certain.

If the cash is definitely not required in the near future then it could be invested in a deposit account for a fixed term of up to three months at a variable rate of interest which is linked to money market rates. This will give a higher rate of return.

Gilt-edged securities

GILT-EDGED SECURITIES or GILTS are marketable British Government securities. They are fixed interest securities and they form the major part of the fixed interest market. Gilts are classified according to their redemption dates as follows:

- Shorts – lives up to five years, eg Treasury 4% 2013
- Mediums – lives from five to fifteen years, eg Treasury 9% 2018
- Longs – lives of more than fifteen years, eg Treasury 6% 2030
- Undated stocks – no redemption date, eg Treasury 2.5%
- Index-linked stocks, eg Treasury IL 2.5% 2011

Gilts prices

Gilts prices are quoted in the financial press every day and are priced for every £100 of stock. For example, on 16 December 2008 the quoted price of Treasury 4.25% 2011 was £104.12. This means that £100 of the gilts could have been purchased for £104.12.

The gilts will be redeemable in 2011 at their nominal value of £100 and as the maturity date moves closer the gilt price will move towards £100.

HOW IT WORKS

The fuel division of SC Fuel and Glass expects to have approximately £50,000 to invest and is considering an investment in Treasury 4.25% 20X9 stock which are currently priced at £104.12.

At this price the division could purchase £48,022 par value of this stock (£50,000/£104.12 × £100).

Income from gilts

Interest is payable on Treasury stock twice a year at the COUPON RATE, which is the rate quoted in the price of the gilt. So for Treasury 4.25% 20Y1 interest for the year is £4.25 per £100 block of stock and is payable in two instalments of £2.125 each at six-month intervals.

Interest yield

The INTEREST YIELD or FLAT RATE YIELD is simply the coupon rate of interest as a percentage of the current price of the gilt. This shows the return on the gilt if it were bought today and held for a year.

HOW IT WORKS

The Treasury 4.25% 20X9 stock which the fuel division is considering investing in is currently priced at £104.12.

$$\text{Interest rate yield} = \frac{£4.25}{£104.12} \times 100 = 4.08\%$$

Task 2

4.5% Treasury stock 2013 are currently quoted at £106.48. What is the interest yield on this stock?

......%   4·23%

Redemption yield

The redemption yield is calculated as:

Interest yield +/– the yield on the gain or loss if held to redemption

The interest yield is calculated as above.

The gain if held to redemption is calculated as:

$$\frac{(\text{Redemption price} - \text{Current price})}{\text{Number of years to redemption}} \times \frac{£100}{\text{Current price}}$$

For example, a fictitious gilt might be Treasury 5% 20Y2 redeemed in five years from today's date and currently priced at £95. It will have the following redemption yield:

$$\text{Interest yield} = \frac{£5}{£95} \times 100 = 5.3\%$$

$$\text{Gain yield} = \frac{(£100 - 95)}{5 \text{ years}} \times \frac{£100}{£95} = 5/5 \times 100/95 = 1.05\%$$

The redemption yield will be 6.35% (5.3 + 1.05)

Gilt prices and interest rates

As gilts are marketable securities, their value fluctuates over time. We have already seen that the price of a gilt is partly determined by the period remaining until maturity. The other factor which affects the price of gilts is the current prevailing market rate of interest.

If general interest rates rise then the value of gilts will tend to fall. The reason for this is that with higher general interest rates the gilts stock must also produce a higher return. The coupon rate of interest cannot be altered but if the market value of the stock falls then the same coupon interest will produce a higher yield.

Similarly, if interest rates fall then the value of gilts will rise.

This is an important factor in the investment decision and therefore any expected changes in the economic and financial environment should be taken into account when investing any surplus funds.

Local authority stocks

In a similar way to government stocks there are a large number of marketable local authority securities which are available for investment purposes. However, local authority stocks are not considered to be quite as secure as central government stocks and the market is not so large which means that local authority stocks have a slightly higher yield than government stocks to compensate.

Certificates of deposit

A CERTIFICATE OF DEPOSIT (CD) is a document issued by a bank or building society which certifies that a certain sum, usually a minimum of £50,000, has been deposited with it to be repaid on a specific date. The term can range from seven days to five years but is usually for six months.

CDs are negotiable instruments which means that they can be bought and sold. Therefore if the holder does not want to wait until the maturity date the CD can be sold in the money market.

CDs offer a good rate of interest, are highly marketable and can be liquidated at any time at the current market rate. The market in CDs is large and active therefore they are an ideal method for investing large cash surpluses.

Bills of exchange

A BILL OF EXCHANGE can be defined as an unconditional order in writing from one person to another requiring the person to whom it is addressed to pay a specified sum of money either on demand (a SIGHT BILL) or at some future date (a TERM BILL). A cheque is a special example of a type of bill of exchange.

Trading in bills of exchange

Most bills of exchange are term bills with a duration or maturity of between two weeks and six months and are of a value of up to £500,000 in any currency. If one company draws a bill on another company this is known as a trade bill. However the market in these is small.

Most bills are BANK BILLS which are bills of exchange drawn and payable by a bank, the most common of these is known as a banker's acceptance. There is an active market in such bills and a company with surplus cash could buy a bill of exchange at a discount and either hold it to maturity or sell it in the market before maturity again at a discount. The difference between the price at which the bill is purchased and the price at which it is sold or it matures is the return to the investor.

Task 3

What is a certificate of deposit (CD)?

A   A financial instrument issued by the government

B   A financial instrument issued by a local authority

C   A financial instrument issued by banks

D   A financial instrument issued by companies

GOVERNMENT MONETARY POLICY

Government monetary policy is a complex area but a brief overview will be given in this section in terms of its relevance to investment and borrowing decisions.

Government monetary policies are the policies that are implemented by the Treasury and the Bank of England in order to deal with the supply of money, interest rates and the availability of credit.

Government market operations

The way in which the government influences the amount of money in the economy is by either restricting or encouraging bank lending. One way of doing this is by the issue of gilts. By selling attractively priced gilts the government takes money away from financial institutions and individuals who pay for these gilts. This takes money out of their bank accounts thereby reducing the banks' asset bases and the amount that the banks can lend.

The use of Treasury Bills by the government also controls bank lending and influences the interest rate. By selling Treasury Bills the government is taking money out of the system and by buying Treasury Bills it can put money back into the system. Through the buying and selling process the government affects the supply and demand levels for investments generally and thereby influences interest rates.

Interest rate policy

The Bank of England, on behalf of the government, controls the short-term interest rate through its operations in the primary money market. When interest rates are increased this reduces the demand for borrowing. This in turn has the effect of reducing consumer demand as less credit is available and the credit that is available is more costly.

Equally, if the Bank of England reduces interest rates this is a boost to the economy as more credit and spending power are available.

DEALING WITH CASH

In this chapter so far we have been considering how to invest any cash surplus that a business may have. However some businesses are cash-based businesses, usually in the retail trade, and you need to be aware of some of the basic requirements for dealing with amounts of cash taken from customers. There are many businesses in the retail sector or manufacturing businesses with a retail outlet which will necessarily have to deal with potentially large amounts of cash on a daily basis before the monies can be banked or otherwise invested.

Security

Cash is a highly risky asset to be holding on the business premises as it can easily be misappropriated or stolen. Therefore, for any cash-based business there must be procedures and policies in place which must be followed to ensure that cash and cheques from customers are secure and are banked as quickly as possible and in full. Increasingly, customers are choosing to pay by debit card, which means there are fewer transactions involving cash (notes and coins) than there used to be.

Procedures for dealing with cash

Any business dealing with cash must have basic security procedures in place to deal with the following aspects:

- Physical safeguards
- Checking for valid payment
- Reconciliation of cash received
- Banking procedures
- Recording procedures

Physical safeguards

Any cash or cheques received must be kept safe at all times and must only be accessible to authorised individuals within the organisation. The cash should be kept under lock and key either in a cash box, lockable till or safe with only authorised individuals having access to the keys.

Checking for valid payment

Payments received in cash will, of course, be valid provided that any notes are not forged. If cheques are accepted as payment then they must be supported by a valid cheque guarantee card and be correctly drawn up, dated and signed. If debit or credit cards are accepted then basic checks should be made on the card and signature and authorisation must be sought for payments which exceed the floor limit.

Reconciliation of cash received

When payments are received in the form of cash, cheques, debit or credit cards then a list of all receipts taken during the day must be kept. This list must then be reconciled at the end of each day to the amount of cash in the till, cash box or safe. The list may be manual as each sale is made or may be automatically recorded on the till roll as each sale is entered.

This reconciliation should not be carried out by the person responsible for making the sales but by some other responsible official. Any discrepancies between the amount of cash recorded as taken during the day and the amount physically left at the end of the day must be investigated.

Banking procedures

Any cash, cheques and debit and credit card vouchers (if the business does not use electronic funds transfer at point of sale, or EFTPOS) should be banked as soon as possible. This not only ensures the physical safety of the cash but also that it cannot be used by employees for unauthorised purposes. It also means that once the money is in the bank it is earning the business the maximum amount of interest. If it is not possible to bank the takings until the following day then either the cash must be left in a locked safe overnight or in the bank's overnight safe.

Recording procedures

For security purposes the paying-in slip for the bank should be made out by someone other than the person paying the money into the bank. The total on the paying-in slip should also be reconciled to the till records or cash list for the day.

Task 4

In a retail business where payment is received from customers by cash, cheque and debit/credit card what reconciliation should be carried out at the end of each day?

A   Reconciliation to bank statement

B   Reconciliation to receivables

C   Reconciliation to cash book

D   Reconciliation to amount of cash/cheques/credit card vouchers

CHAPTER OVERVIEW

- If a cash surplus is identified then it should normally be invested to earn profits for the business – when considering potential investments thought should be given to risk, return and liquidity.

- There are many types of investment that would be suitable for surplus cash and these include bank deposit accounts, gilt-edged securities, local authority stocks, certificates of deposit and bills of exchange.

- Government monetary policies are the policies implemented by the Treasury and the Bank of England in order to control the supply of money, interest rates and the availability of credit.

- Much of government monetary policy is carried out through the issuing or buying of gilts and Treasury Bills in order to control the money supply and interest rates.

- In a business where large amounts of cash/cheques/debit and credit card payments are received from customers, procedures should be in place to ensure that the cash is physically secure, controlled and paid into the bank as soon as possible.

KEY WORDS

Cash surplus – surplus cash held in the business's current account

Risk – the chance of making a loss

Return – any income and/or capital gain on an investment

Income return – interest or dividend received

Capital return – increase/decrease in market value of an investment

Liquidity – the ease and speed with which an investment can be converted into cash

Gilt-edged securities/gilts – marketable British government securities

Coupon rate – interest rate included in the title of the gilts

Interest yield/flat rate yield – income return on the gilts if held for one year

Redemption yield – return on the gilts if held to maturity

Certificate of deposit – a document issued by a bank which certifies that a certain sum has been deposited with it to be repaid on a specific date – a negotiable instrument and highly marketable

Bill of exchange – unconditional order in writing from one person to another requiring the person to whom it is addressed to pay a specified sum

Sight bill – bill of exchange payable on demand

Term bill – bill of exchange payable at some future date

Bank bill – bill of exchange drawn and payable by a bank

TEST YOUR LEARNING

Test 1

Use the picklists to complete the following sentence.

A dividend from an investment is an example of [revenue/capital] return and an increase in the value of an investment is an example of [revenue/capital] return.

Test 2

The redemption yield on a gilt-edged security is the income if it were purchased today and held for a year.

True or false?

FALSE

Test 3

If there is a general rise in interest rates what affect is this likely to have on the price of gilt-edged securities?

Tick the correct answer.

Increase

Decrease ✓

Test 4

"An unconditional order in writing from one person to another requiring the person to whom it is addressed to pay a specified sum of money either on demand or at some future date."

What sort of investment is this a description of?

A   Gilt edged security

B   Bill of exchange

C   Certificate of deposit

D   Local authority loan

chapter 8:
MONITORING CASH FLOWS

chapter coverage 📖

The cash budget is not just a tool for predicting cash shortfalls or cash surpluses but can also be used to monitor and control cash-inflows and cash outflows. It can be used to compare actual cash flows to those that were budgeted and to quantify any deviations from the budgeted cash flows so that appropriate courses of action can be taken by management.

The topics covered are:

✍ Monitoring cash flows

✍ Using cash budgets

MONITORING CASH FLOWS

We have already seen that one of the important roles of management is that of control of operations and transactions. One way of controlling the operations of the business is to compare the actual effects of the operations to those that were anticipated in the business plans.

It has already been seen that cash is a vital element of any business and therefore it is an important management role to compare the actual cash flows for a period to the expected cash flows as shown in the cash flow forecast. If there are significant differences between the actual and expected cash flows then management should investigate the reasons for these differences and consider any action necessary to ensure that cash flows and cash balances revert to plan.

There are two main methods of comparing the actual cash flows and position to the budgeted cash flows and budgeted cash balance:

- Comparison of each individual cash flow
- Reconciliation of the actual cash balance to the budgeted cash balance

Comparison of individual cash flows

Under this method of monitoring the actual cash flows of a business, for each individual line of the cash forecast the actual cash flow for the period is compared with the budgeted cash flow and the difference is recorded. This difference is often known as the VARIANCE.

HOW IT WORKS

Given below is the cash budget for the fuel division of SC for the month of June together with the actual cash flows for the month.

Cash budget: June

	Budgeted cash flows £	Actual cash flows £
Receipts:		
Cash sales	110,000	106,500
Receipts from credit customers	655,000	633,000
Proceeds from sale of non-current (fixed) assets	–	15,000
Total receipts	765,000	754,500

Payments:

Payments to credit suppliers	550,000	589,000
Wages	108,000	108,000
Rent	10,000	10,500
Advertising	12,000	9,000
Purchase of non-current (fixed) assets	–	27,000
Dividend payment	20,000	20,000
Total payments	700,000	763,500
Net cash flow	65,000	(9,000)
Opening cash balance	10,000	10,000
Closing cash balance	75,000	1,000

Note how the actual net cash flow is a cash outflow, shown in brackets, as the total payments in the month were greater than the total receipts.

We can now compare the actual and budgeted figures for each line of the cash budget to discover the differences or variances.

	Budgeted cash flows	Actual cash flows	Variance
	£	£	£
Cash sales	110,000	106,500	(3,500)
Receipts from credit customers	655,000	633,000	(22,000)
Proceeds from sale of non-current (fixed) assets	–	15,000	15,000
Total receipts	765,000	754,500	
Payments:			
Payments to credit suppliers	550,000	589,000	(39,000)
Wages	108,000	108,000	–
Rent	10,000	10,500	(500)
Advertising	12,000	9,000	3,000
Purchase of non-current (fixed) assets	–	27,000	(27,000)
Dividend payment	20,000	20,000	–
Total payments	700,000	763,500	
Net cash flow	65,000	(9,000)	(74,000)
Opening cash balance	10,000	10,000	–
Closing cash balance	75,000	1,000	(74,000)

Any difference which is good news, such as receipts being higher than budgeted or payments being lower than budgeted, are known as FAVOURABLE VARIANCES.

Any differences which are bad news, where receipts are less than budgeted or payments are greater than budgeted, are known as ADVERSE VARIANCES. The adverse variances are shown in brackets.

Further investigation

At this stage it is likely that some or all of these variances would be investigated.

Receipts

Cash sales	–	why are these less than budgeted?
Receipts from customers	–	why are these less than budgeted?
Sale of non-current (fixed) asset	–	this is an unexpected receipt but why has the sale taken place if it was not planned for?

Payments

Payments to credit suppliers	–	why are these greater than budgeted?
Rent	–	this is probably a rent increase that was not included in the forecast
Advertising	–	why are these costs lower than budgeted?
Purchase of non-current (fixed) assets	–	why has this taken place when it was not budgeted for? Was the purchase to replace the non-current asset that was sold?

The overall effect of all of these variances from the cash forecast figures is that the net cash flow for the period is £74,000 lower than anticipated and the forecast cash balance is therefore £74,000 lower than anticipated.

Management action to be taken

Having discovered the variances between the actual cash flows and the budgeted cash flows management may wish to take actions to try to bring the cash position back in line with the budgeted position. What possible actions might they take with the fuel division of SC?

Receipts from credit customers	–	credit control might be improved to encourage earlier payments from customers
Payments to credit suppliers	–	these may be delayed
Purchase of non-current (fixed) assets	–	these should be considered to determine if they are necessary and if there is another form of financing that does not require so much cash to be spent immediately

Task 1

Receipts from credit customers for a period were £186,000 compared to the budgeted figure of £168,000. Is this a favourable or an adverse variance? (Tick the correct answer)

Favourable ✓

Adverse ☐

Reconciliation of actual cash balance to budgeted cash balance

This method of comparing actual to budgeted cash flows uses many of the same calculations as in the method above but presents the final information in a slightly different manner. Again each line in the cash flow forecast is compared to the actual figure and the variance is calculated. However, these variances are then used to reconcile the final actual cash balance to the final budgeted cash balance.

HOW IT WORKS

Again we will use the cash flow forecast and actual figures for June for the fuel division of SC.

	June	
	Budgeted cash flows	Actual cash flows
	£	£
Receipts:		
Cash sales	110,000	106,500
Receipts from credit customers	655,000	633,000
Proceeds from sale of non-current (fixed) assets	–	15,000
Total receipts	765,000	754,500
Payments:		
Payments to credit suppliers	550,000	589,000
Wages	108,000	108,000
Rent	10,000	10,500
Advertising	12,000	9,000
Purchase of non-current (fixed) assets	–	27,000
Dividend payment	20,000	20,000
Total payments	700,000	763,500
Net cash flow	65,000	(9,000)
Opening cash balance	10,000	10,000
Closing cash balance	75,000	1,000

Again, the variance for each line of the cash flow forecast is calculated:

June

	Budgeted cash flows	Actual cash flows	Variance
	£	£	£
Receipts:			
Cash sales	110,000	106,500	(3,500)
Receipts from credit customers	655,000	633,000	(22,000)
Proceeds from sale of non-current (fixed) assets	–	15,000	15,000
Total receipts	765,000	754,500	
Payments:			
Payments to credit suppliers	550,000	589,000	(39,000)
Wages	108,000	108,000	–
Rent	10,000	10,500	(500)
Advertising	12,000	9,000	3,000
Purchase of non-current (fixed) assets	–	27,000	(27,000)
Dividend payment	20,000	20,000	–
Total payments	700,000	763,500	
Net cash flow	65,000	(9,000)	(74,000)
Opening cash balance	10,000	10,000	–
Closing cash balance	75,000	1,000	(74,000)

These figures are then used to explain why the actual cash balance at the end of June was £1,000 when it had been budgeted to be £75,000.

This is normally done by starting with the budgeted cash balance and adding any favourable variances and deducting any adverse variances.

June – reconciliation of actual cash balance to budgeted cash balance

	£
Budgeted cash balance	75,000
Shortfall in cash sales	(3,500)
Shortfall in receipts from customers	(22,000)
Additional receipt from sale of non-current (fixed) asset	15,000
Additional payments to credit suppliers	(39,000)
Additional rent	(500)
Lower advertising cost	3,000
Additional non-current (fixed) asset purchase	(27,000)
Actual cash balance	1,000

Task 2

If the budgeted cash balance is to be reconciled to the actual cash balance a variance is added to the budgeted cash balance?

True or False?   FALSE

USING CASH BUDGETS

As well as using a cash budget to monitor any differences between actual cash flows and what had been anticipated, the cash budget can also be used for other purposes.

Identifying cash surpluses or deficits

As we have seen if a cash budget is prepared for a number of periods in advance then the anticipated cash balance at the end of each of those periods can be forecast. The management of the business can then plan ahead as to how to invest any anticipated cash surplus and how to fund any anticipated cash deficit.

Taking action to improve the budgeted position

A cash budget shows what the cash position is expected to be given the current and planned circumstances and operations of the business. However if the cash budget indicates an excessive surplus or, perhaps more importantly, an overdraft which exceeds the agreed limit, then the advance warning gives management the opportunity to change policies or operating practices in order to improve the position that is indicated in the cash budget.

Suppose that an excessive overdraft was predicted by the cash budget. The types of actions that could be taken include:

- Improving credit control procedures to ensure money is received from credit customers sooner

- Increasing the proportion of cash sales in comparison to credit sales

- Selling surplus non-current (fixed) assets

- Increasing the period of credit taken from suppliers therefore paying suppliers later

- Negotiating credit terms for expenses that are currently paid in cash

- Delaying payments for non-current (fixed) assets

- Changing the method of financing the purchase of non-current (fixed) assets

- Waiving or delaying dividend payments or drawings for a sole trader

Discretionary and non-discretionary payments

Some care has to be taken when making suggestions as to how to improve a forecast cash flow position as there are some payments that must be made on time known as NON-DISCRETIONARY PAYMENTS, whereas there are others, DISCRETIONARY PAYMENTS, which can validly be delayed.

HOW IT WORKS

SC Fuel and Glass has now prepared its cash budgets for the fuel division for the quarter ending 30 September on the basis that the opening cash balance is the actual closing balance of £1,000 at the end of June. The company has an agreed overdraft limit of £50,000.

The cash budget for the three months to 30 September appears as follows:

	July £	August £	Sept £
Receipts:			
Cash sales	80,000	94,000	98,000
Receipts from credit customers	612,000	588,000	561,000
Proceeds from sale of non-current (fixed) assets	–	–	22,000
Total receipts	692,000	682,000	681,000

Payments:

Payments to credit suppliers	520,000	500,000	520,000
Wages	108,000	108,000	108,000
Rent	10,500	10,500	10,500
Advertising	12,000	2,000	2,000
Purchase of non-current (fixed) assets	25,000	37,000	–
VAT	22,000		
Corporation tax	–	90,000	
Total payments	697,500	747,500	640,500
Net cash flow	(5,500)	(65,500)	40,500
Opening cash balance	1,000	(4,500)	(70,000)
Closing cash balance	(4,500)	(70,000)	(29,500)

There is an anticipated overdraft at the end of each of the three months but the main problem is that in August the agreed overdraft limit is exceeded by £20,000. Is there anything that can be done to improve this position and try to keep the division within its agreed overdraft limit?

Receipts

Cash sales receipts	–	there is probably little that can be done over such a short space of time to improve the cash sales position
Receipts from credit customers	–	it might be possible to tighten credit control procedures and collect money earlier from these customers
Sale of non-current (fixed) assets	–	if this asset is surplus to requirements it may be possible to sell it in July or August or if it is being sold on credit to collect the money sooner

Payments

Payments to credit suppliers	–	it may be possible to extend the period of credit to suppliers and pay them later thereby improving the cash position
Wages	–	wages are non-discretionary and must be paid in full and on time
Rent	–	it is unlikely that there could be any renegotiation of the payment terms for the rent
Advertising	–	there is a large cost in July. Could this be postponed or alternatively paid for over a number of months rather than in one go?
Purchase of non-current (fixed) assets	–	large amounts of purchases in July and August. It may be possible to delay these purchases, negotiate credit terms for the payment or take out a bank loan rather than paying in cash
VAT	–	this is a non-discretionary payment and must be paid when due otherwise financial penalties will be incurred
Corporation tax	–	this is a non-discretionary payment and must be paid when due otherwise financial penalties will be incurred

Task 3

Complete the table by choosing each transaction to correctly match the type of payment from the list below.

Type of payment	Description
Discretionary	
Non-discretionary	

Amount due to HM Revenue and Customs   N D

Dividend   D

Capital expenditure   D

Corporation tax   N D

Payment to credit suppliers N D

Drawings   D

CHAPTER OVERVIEW

- As part of the management role of control it is important to compare the actual cash flows for a period to the budgeted or forecast cash flows – this can be done by calculating variances on a line by line basis or by reconciling the actual cash balance to the budgeted cash balance.

- Once the variances between actual and budgeted cash flows have been determined they may be investigated and appropriate actions taken.

- A cash budget, once prepared, can indicate to management future cash surpluses or deficits and can also indicate areas where procedures and policies can be altered or improved in order to improve the cash position.

KEY WORDS

Variance – the difference between actual results and budgeted results

Favourable variances – variances which represent greater income or less expense than budgeted

Adverse variances – variances which represent less income or greater expense than budgeted

Discretionary payments – payments which can validly be cancelled or delayed

Non-discretionary payments – payments which must be made on time for the business to continue

TEST YOUR LEARNING

Test 1

Given below is the cash budget for Glenn Security Systems for the month of May together with the actual cash flows for the month.

(a) Identify and quantify three significant differences/variances between the actual cash flow for the month and the budgeted cash flow

-
-
-

(b) Suggest three actions that the company could have taken to avoid using its overdraft facility

-
-
-

Cash budget May

	Budget £	Actual £
Cash sales receipts	43,000	45,000
Credit sales receipts	256,000	231,000
Credit suppliers	(176,000)	(189,000)
Wages	(88,000)	(88,000)
Overheads	(43,200)	(44,500)
Capital expenditure	-	(40,000)
Movement for the month	(8,200)	(85,500)
Bank b/f	53,400	52,100
Bank c/f	45,200	(33,400)

Test 2

Given below is the cash budget for Glenn Security Systems for the month of May together with the actual cash flows for the month.

	Budget £	Actual £
Cash sales receipts	43,000	45,000
Credit sales receipts	256,000	231,000
Payments to credit suppliers	(176,000)	(189,000)
Wages	(88,000)	(88,000)
Overheads	(43,200)	(44,500)
Capital expenditure	–	(40,000)
Movement for the month	(8,200)	(85,500)
Bank b/f	53,400	52,100
Bank c/f	45,200	(33,400)

Prepare a reconciliation of budgeted cash flow with actual cash flow for the month.

	£
Budgeted cash balance at 31 May	45.200
Surplus/shortfall in receipts from cash sales	2000
Surplus/shortfall in receipts from credit sales	(25000)
Surplus/shortfall in payments to credit suppliers	(13000)
Increase/decrease in overheads	(1300)
Increase/decrease in capital expenditure	(40,000)
Lower opening cash balance	(1300)
Actual cash balance	(33400)

Test 3

Given below are the cash budgets for the quarter ending 30 June for Davies Engineering. The company has an agreed overdraft facility of £20,000.

Cash budget

	April £	May £	June £
Receipts:			
Cash sales	64,000	75,000	78,000
Receipts from credit customers	489,000	470,000	449,000
Proceeds from sale of non-current (fixed) assets	–	10,000	–
Total receipts	553,000	555,000	527,000
Payments:			
Payments to credit suppliers	426,000	437,000	425,000
Wages	84,000	84,000	84,000
Rent	8,000	8,000	8,000
Capital expenditure	26,000	28,000	–
VAT	–	12,200	
Training costs	20,000		
Repairs and maintenance	10,400		
Total payments	574,400	569,200	517,000
Net cash flow	(21,400)	(14,200)	10,000
Opening cash balance	2,600	(18,800)	(33,000)
Closing cash balance	(18,800)	(33,000)	(23,000)

Which of the following courses of action could improve the cash forecast position and keep the company within its agreed overdraft limit?

(i)   Improve credit collection and speed up receipts from credit customers
(ii)   Sell non-current (fixed) asset earlier or arrange for cash to be received earlier
(iii)   Increase credit period taken from suppliers by paying later
(iv)   Delay capital expenditure in April and May
(v)   Finance capital expenditure differently eg bank loan
(vi)   Delay training courses
(vii)   Negotiate credit terms for repairs and maintenance costs

A   (i), (iii), (iv), (vii)
B   (i), (ii), (v), (vi), (vii)
C   (i), (ii), (v), (vii)
D   (i), (iii), (iv), (v), (vi), (vii)

CHAPTER 1 Liquidity

1 B

$$\text{Average inventory (stock)} = \frac{£13,500 + £17,000}{2}$$

$$= £15,250$$

$$\text{Inventory (stock) turnover period} = \frac{£15,250 \times 365}{£99,000}$$

$$= 56 \text{ days}$$

2 C

Inventory (stock) turnover period	84 days
Receivables (debtors) collection period	51 days
	135 days
Less: payables (creditors) payment period	(43 days)
Working capital cycle	92 days

CHAPTER 2 Cash flow and profit

1 C

This is the only one which affects profit in the same way as the cash of the business as the wages are charged to profit and paid in the same period.

2 (a) cash transaction
   (b) cash transaction
   (c) credit transaction
   (d) credit transaction

3

Sales 125,000 + 14,000 – 10,000	£129,000
Purchases 80,000 + 8,000 – 11,000	£77,000
Operating expenses 15,000 + 3,000 – 2,000	£16,000

CHAPTER 3   Cash receipts and payments

1

Type of receipt or payment	Description
Exceptional receipt	Insurance claim receipt
Exceptional payment	Hire of machinery due to breakdown of own machine

2   **November receipts**

		£
August sales	320,000 × 25%	80,000
September sales	360,000 × 35%	126,000
October sales	400,000 × 40%	160,000
Total November receipts		**366,000**

3   **October receipts**

		£
August sales	120,000 × 40%	48,000
September sales	100,000 × 50%	50,000
October sales	150,000 × 10% x 97.5%	14,625
Total cash receipts		**112,625**

CHAPTER 4   Forecasting future cash receipts and payments

1

	Monthly costs	3 month moving average
	£'000	£'000
January	129	
February	138	134
March	135	138
April	142	142
May	150	148
June	153	150
July	148	151
August	151	154
September	162	159
October	165	166
November	172	167
December	164	

2   Increase in trend $= 369 - 319$

$= 50$

Average increase in trend over nine changes

$= 5.6$ per quarter

20X9	Forecast trend	Seasonal variation	Forecast sales
	£'000	£'000	£'000
Q1	$369 + (2 \times 5.6)$	-21.3	358.9
Q2	$369 + (3 \times 5.6)$	-27.6	358.2
Q3	$369 + (4 \times 5.6)$	+14.1	405.5
Q4	$369 + (5 \times 5.6)$	+34.8	431.8

3

	Expected sales value £
October 43,000 × £95	4,085,000
November 40,000 × £95 × 1.05	3,990,000

4

	Expected purchases value £
October 100,000 × £15.80 × 1.012	1,598,960
November 100,000 × £15.80 ×1.012 × 1.012	1,618,148

5   A

June 200,000 × 196.4/195.3 = £201,126

CHAPTER 5   Preparing cash budgets

1   **Cash budget – November**

	£
Cash receipts:	
Cash sales	64,000
Credit sales (Nov 238,000 × 40% × 98%) + (Oct 216,000 × 60%)	222,896
Total cash receipts	**286,896**
Cash payments:	
Purchases on credit	-144,000
Wages and salaries	-80,000
Overheads	-50,000
Dividend	-20,000
Total cash payments	**-294,000**
Net cash flow	-7,104
Opening balance	-10,200
Closing balance	-17,304

2

		Period 3	Period 4	Period 5
Period 1	(21,200 x 70%)	14,840		
Period 2	(24,000 x 30%)	7,200		
Period 2	(24,000 x 70%)		16,800	
Period 3	(24,550 x 30%)		7,365	
Period 3	(24,550 x 70%)			17,185
Period 4	(27,350 x 30%)			8,205
		22,040	24,165	25,390

CHAPTER 6   Managing cash shortages

1   The main advantages of financial intermediation are:

- Small amounts deposited by savers can be combined to provide larger loan packages to businesses

- Short-term savings can be transferred into long-term borrowings

- Search costs are reduced as companies seeking loan finance can approach a bank directly rather than finding individuals to lend to them

- Risk is reduced as an individual's savings are not tied up with one individual borrower directly

2   C

3   A secondary money market is one where existing financial instruments are traded.

4   D

5   D

CHAPTER 7   Managing surplus funds

1   The general relationship between risk and return with investments is that the higher the risk the higher the return OR that the lower the risk the lower the return.

2   Interest yield $= \dfrac{4.50}{106.48} \times 100$

$= 4.23\%$

3   C

4   D

CHAPTER 8   Monitoring cash flows

1   Favourable

       Adverse

2   False

       An adverse variance is subtracted from the budgeted cash balance in order to reconcile to the actual cash balance.

3

Type of payment	Description
Discretionary	Dividend
	Capital expenditure
	Drawings
Non-discretionary	Amount due to HM Revenue and Customs
	Corporation tax
	Payment to credit suppliers

TEST YOUR LEARNING – ANSWERS

CHAPTER 1   Liquidity

1   C

Inventory (stock) turnover	=	$\dfrac{£68,000}{£593,000}$ × 365 =	42 days
Receivables (debtors) collection	=	$\dfrac{£102,000}{£790,000}$ × 365 =	47 days
Payables (creditors) payment	=	$\dfrac{£57,000}{£593,000}$ × 365 =	(35 days)
Operating cycle		=	54 days

2   ▪ Cash in hand
    ▪ Bank current account
    ▪ Bank deposit account

3   The three main principles are <u>security, liquidity, profitability.</u>

4   Over-capitalisation

CHAPTER 2   Cash flow and profit

1   Although it is important for a business to <u>make a profit</u> it can be argued that it is even more important for a business to <u>have a healthy cash balance</u> in order to be able to pay amounts when they are due.

2   Prepayment of rent   ✓

   Purchase of a non-current (fixed) asset   ✓

   Purchases of inventory(stock) for cash   ☐

   Depreciation   ✓

   Cash sales   ☐

3

	£
Sales receipts 720,000 + 60,000 – 75,000	705,000
Purchases payments 471,000 + 70,000 – 104,000	437,000
Expenses payments 130,000 + 5,000 – 13,000 – 64,000	58,000
Depreciation (non-cash expense)	0

CHAPTER 3 Cash receipts and payments

1   **Forecast cash receipts**

		January	February	March
		£	£	£
Cash sales	10% of sales	70,000	73,000	76,000
Credit sales	720,000 × 40%	288,000		
	700,000 × 40%		280,000	
	730,000 × 40%			292,000
	750,000 × 45%	337,500		
	720,000 × 45%		324,000	
	700,000 × 45%			315,000
Total receipts from sales		**695,500**	**677,000**	**683,000**

2   **Forecast cash payments**

		January	February	March
		£	£	£
October purchases	592,500 × 15%	88,875		
November purchases	562,500 × 65%	365,625		
	562,500 × 15%		84,375	
December purchases	540,000 × 20% × 98%	105,840		
	540,000 × 65%		351,000	
	540,000 × 15%			81,000
January purchases	525,000 × 20% × 98%		102,900	
	525,000 × 65%			341,250
February purchases	547,400 × 20% × 98%			107,310
Total payments for purchases		**560,340**	**538,275**	**529,560**

CHAPTER 4   Forecasting future cash receipts and payments

1

		Takings	5 day moving average
		£	£
Week 1	Tuesday	560	
	Wednesday	600	
	Thursday	630	720
	Friday	880	716
	Saturday	930	714
Week 2	Tuesday	540	716
	Wednesday	590	710
	Thursday	640	712
	Friday	850	714
	Saturday	940	708
Week 3	Tuesday	550	700
	Wednesday	560	704
	Thursday	600	710
	Friday	870	
	Saturday	970	

2   (a)

		Production in units	Trend in units
Week 1	Monday	1,400	
	Tuesday	1,600	
	Wednesday	1,800	1,630
	Thursday	1,800	1,626
	Friday	1,550	1,630
Week 2	Monday	1,380	1,636
	Tuesday	1,620	1,638
	Wednesday	1,830	1,628
	Thursday	1,810	1,642
	Friday	1,500	1,648
Week 3	Monday	1,450	1,652
	Tuesday	1,650	1,658
	Wednesday	1,850	1,672
	Thursday	1,840	
	Friday	1,570	

(b) Increase in trend 1,672 – 1,630   = 42

   Number of increases   = 10

   Average increase   = 4.2 units per day

(c)

Day	Trend in units	Seasonal variation	Forecast volume in units
Monday	1,672 + (3 × 4.2)	× 86.1%	**1,450**
Tuesday	1,672 + (4 × 4.2)	× 99.2%	**1,675**
Wednesday	1,672 + (5 × 4.2)	× 111.1%	**1,881**
Thursday	1,672 + (6 × 4.2)	× 110.5%	**1,875**
Friday	1,672 + (7 × 4.2)	× 93.1%	**1,584**

3

	Sales in units	Price per unit	Cash inflow	Purchases in units	Price per unit	Cash outflow
		£	£		£	£
Jan	4,800	35	**168,000**	5,200	20	**104,000**
Feb	5,000	35 × 1.08	**189,000**	5,800	20 × 1.05	**121,800**
Mar	5,600	35 × 1.08	**211,680**	5,500	20 × 1.05	**115,500**

4 D

December cash payment is November overheads.

November overheads £160,000 × 1.0175 × 1.0175 = £165,649

5

	Index calculation	Expected price £
October	£10.80 × 151.6/148.5	11.03
November	£10.80 × 154.2/148.5	11.21
December	£10.80 × 158.7/148.5	11.54

CHAPTER 5   Preparing cash budgets

1   (a)   **Sales receipts**

	October	November	December
	£	£	£
September sales 360,000 × 80%	288,000		
October sales 400,000 × 20% × 95%	76,000		
October sales 400,000 × 80%		320,000	
November sales 450,000 × 20% × 95%		85,500	
November sales 450,000 × 80%			360,000
December sales 460,000 × 20% × 95%			87,400
Total receipts from sales	**364,000**	**405,500**	**447,400**

(b)   **Purchases payments**

	October	November	December
	£	£	£
August purchases 200,000 × 70%	140,000		
September purchases 220,000 × 30%	66,000		
September purchases 220,000 × 70%		154,000	
October purchases 240,000 × 30%		72,000	
October purchases 240,000 × 70%			168,000
November purchases 270,000 × 30%			81,000
Total payments for purchases	**206,000**	**226,000**	**249,000**

(c) **General overheads**

	October	November	December
	£	£	£
September overheads (30,000 – 5,000) × 20%	5,000		
October overheads (30,000 – 5,000) × 80%	20,000		
October overheads (30,000 – 5,000) × 20%		5,000	
November overheads (36,000 – 5,000) × 80%		24,800	
November overheads (36,000 – 5,000) × 20%			6,200
December overheads (36,000 – 5,000) × 80%			24,800
Total payment for overheads	**25,000**	**29,800**	**31,000**

(d) **Cash budget for the quarter ending 31 December**

	October	November	December
	£	£	£
Cash receipts			
Sales proceeds from equipment		4,000	
Receipts from sales	364,000	405,500	447,400
Total receipts	**364,000**	**409,500**	**447,400**
Cash payments			
Payments for purchases	-206,000	-226,000	-249,000
Wages	-42,000	-42,000	-42,000
General overheads	-25,000	-29,800	-31,000
Selling expenses	-18,000	-20,000	-22,500
New equipment	0	-40,000	0
Overdraft interest	-500	0	0
Total payments	**-291,500**	**-357,800**	**-344,500**
Net cash flow	**72,500**	**51,700**	**102,900**
Opening balance	**-50,000**	**22,500**	**74,200**
Closing balance	**22,500**	**74,200**	**177,100**

2 (a) **Sales receipts**

	October	November	December
	£	£	£
August sales 7,000 × £60 × 40%	168,000		
September sales 7,200 × £60 × 60%	259,200		
September sales 7,200 × £60 × 40%		172,800	
October sales 6,800 × £60 × 60%		244,800	
October sales 6,800 × £60 × 40%			163,200
November sales 7,400 × £60 × 60%			266,400
Total receipts from sales	**427,200**	**417,600**	**429,600**

(b) **Payments – £**

	October	November	December
	£	£	£
September purchases 172,800 × 60%	103,680		
October purchases 163,200 × 40%	65,280		
October purchases 163,200 × 60%		97,920	
November purchases 178,800 × 40%		71,520	
November purchases 178,800 × 60%			107,280
December purchases 175,200 × 40%			70,080
Total payments for purchases	**168,960**	**169,440**	**177,360**

(c) **Cash budget for the quarter ending 31 December**

	October	November	December
	£	£	£
Cash receipts			
Sales	427,200	417,600	429,600
Cash payments			
Purchases	-168,960	-169,440	-177,360
Wages	-100,500	-109,500	-111,000
Production overheads	-65,280	-71,520	-70,080
General overheads	-52,000	-52,000	-58,000
Total payments	**-386,740**	**-402,460**	**-416,440**
Net cash flow	**40,460**	**15,140**	**13,160**
Opening balance	**20,000**	**60,460**	**75,600**
Closing balance	**60,460**	**75,600**	**88,760**

CHAPTER 6 Managing cash shortages

1 A

2 B

3 LIBOR stands for <u>London inter-bank offered rate.</u>

4 Floating charge required

   Interest charged only on amount of facility used   ✓

   Repayable on demand

5 B

A medium-term loan from a bank would probably be the most appropriate source of finance for the purchase of the shares in B Ltd. Provided that the intention is to keep the shares for some time and therefore to benefit from income from those shares in that period then the loan would match the time scale of the investment in the company and the income could be used to service the loan.

6 The three main repayment patterns of repaying a loan are:

- Bullet repayments
- Balloon repayments
- Amortising repayments

7 A fixed charge is security against the <u>non-current (fixed) assets</u> of a business.

CHAPTER 7 Managing surplus funds

1 A dividend from an investment is an example of <u>revenue</u> return and an increase in the value of an investment is an example of <u>capital</u> return.

2 False

The interest yield shows the income return on the gilt if it were purchased today and held for a year. However the redemption yield gives an overall return on the gilt if it were held to maturity.

3 Increase

   Decrease   ✓

If interest rates rise then the price of gilts will be expected to fall in order to maintain an adequate return on the investment.

4 B

CHAPTER 8   Monitoring cash flows

1
                                                                                    £

(a)   Credit sales receipts   25,000 (A)

      Payments to credit suppliers   13,000 (A)

      Capital expenditure   40,000 (A)

(b)   Improve credit collection to speed up receipt of money from customers

      Lengthen the period of credit taken from suppliers

      Postpone the purchase of non-current (fixed) assets

2   Reconciliation of budgeted cash balance to actual cash balance

	£
Budgeted cash balance at 31 May	45,200
Surplus/shortfall in receipts from cash sales (45,000 – 43,000)	2,000
Surplus/shortfall in receipts from credit sales (256,000 – 231,000)	(25,000)
Surplus/shortfall in payments to suppliers (189,000 – 176,000)	(13,000)
Increase/decrease in overheads (44,500 – 43,200)	(1,300)
Increase/decrease in capital expenditure	(40,000)
Lower opening cash balance (53,400 – 52,100)	(1,300)
Actual cash balance	(33,400)

3   D

INDEX

Notes

Notes

REVIEW FORM

How have you used this Text?
(Tick one box only)

☐ Home study

☐ On a course_____

☐ Other _____

Why did you decide to purchase this Text? *(Tick one box only)*

☐ Have used BPP Texts in the past

☐ Recommendation by friend/colleague

☐ Recommendation by a college lecturer

☐ Saw advertising

☐ Other _____

During the past six months do you recall seeing/receiving either of the following?
(Tick as many boxes as are relevant)

☐ Our advertisement in Accounting Technician

☐ Our Publishing Catalogue

Which (if any) aspects of our advertising do you think are useful?
(Tick as many boxes as are relevant)

☐ Prices and publication dates of new editions

☐ Information on Text content

☐ Details of our free online offering

☐ None of the above

Your ratings, comments and suggestions would be appreciated on the following areas of this Text.

	Very useful	Useful	Not useful
Introductory section	☐	☐	☐
Quality of explanations	☐	☐	☐
How it works	☐	☐	☐
Chapter tasks	☐	☐	☐
Chapter Overviews	☐	☐	☐
Test your learning	☐	☐	☐
Index	☐	☐	☐

	Excellent	Good	Adequate	Poor
Overall opinion of this Text	☐	☐	☐	☐

Do you intend to continue using BPP Products?   Yes ☐   No ☐

Please note any further comments and suggestions/errors on the reverse of this page. The author of this edition can be e-mailed at: suedexter@bpp.com

Please return to: Sue Dexter, Publishing Director, BPP Learning Media Ltd, FREEPOST, London, W12 8BR.

REVIEW FORM (continued)

TELL US WHAT YOU THINK

Please note any further comments and suggestions/errors below.